Welcome

Hands up anyone who's used a microwave to speed-cook a baked potato, or a bread maker as a shortcut to homemade bread! Handy kitchen gadgets are just part and parcel of the way we live today. I love things quick and simple, but with the same results as half a day spent slaving away...

Take scrapbooking. I have loved to scrapbook since 'way back when' – young, single and free to while away hours frivolously. I am now a busy mother of four, who juggles writing, teaching and working in the growing scrapbooking industry, alongside school runs, clubs and domestics chores. I am more harassed, my hair never looks perfect, and I have simply hundreds of photos of my children smeared in Marmite or chocolate spread.

My time spent scrapbooking is limited and I am definitely always looking for the quick and simple shortcuts, without skimping on the finished result. I want a banquet – but microwaved!

So here it is, a book filled with inspiration and the cheats and secrets that our design team use to get their projects done. I love the idea that if you plan, organise and scrap smarter, you can accomplish a whole album in just a weekend.

It has been really exciting to work on this project with a huge range of talented designers from both sides of 'the Pond'. Opening boxes filled with layouts has been like Christmas every day! I am sure their work will inspire you, and their design secrets motivate you to scrapbook in half the time.

If you are anything like me, you will love this book. Have fun with the ideas, but most of all, **have a go**!

Becks Fagg
Mother, Editor & Scrapbooker

EDITORIAL
Managing Editor Michelle Grant
Editor Becks Fagg
becks.fagg@practicalpublishing.co.uk
Editorial Assistant Lindsey Hopkins
lindsey.hopkins@practicalpublishing.co.uk
Sub-editors Lee Jepson, Kate Timmins
Art & Design Craig Chubb
Additional Design Roy Birch, Tym Leckey
Photographer Rachel Burgess

THE DESIGN TEAM
Mandy Anderson, Michelle Baker, Shauna Berglund-Immel, Jenni Bowlin, Paul Browning, Nicola Clarke, Teresa Collins, Candice Cook, Mandi Coombs, Brenda Cosgrove, Alison Docherty, Nena Earl, Becky Fleck, Kelly Goree, Anne Hafermann, Debbie Hill, Michelle Hill, Tim Holtz, Kim Kesti, Marla Kress, Annette Lauts, Theresa Lundström, Anita MacDonald, Faye Morrow Bell, Missy Neal, Natalie O'Shea, Stacey Panassidi, Rozanne Paxman, Debi Potter, Sue Roberts, Natasha Roe, Katie Shanahan-Jones, Shalae Tippetts, Kellene Truby, Janna Wilson, Kirsty Wiseman

PUBLISHING
Operations Manager Glen Urquhart
Marketing Manager Iain Anderson
iain.anderson@practicalpublishing.co.uk
Accounts Manager Karen Battrick
Circulation Manager David Wren
Publisher Robin Wilkinson

CONTACT
Practical Publishing International Ltd,
Europa House,
Adlington Park, Adlington,
Macclesfield, Cheshire,
UK SK10 4NP
info@practicalpublishing.co.uk
www.practicalpublishing.co.uk
Tel: 0870 242 7038
Fax: 01625 855 011

Scrapbooking in a weekend
(ISBN 978-0-9551371-2-9)
Published by Practical Publishing International Ltd

Contents

All you need to know

Galleries

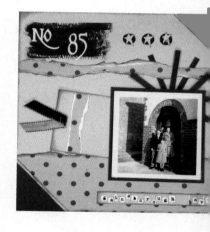

Getting Started

If you are new to the hobby of scrapbooking, use our essential 'at a glance' guide to stock up on the supplies you need to get you started

"We shall not fail or falter; we shall not weaken or tire… Give us the tools and we will finish the job." - Sir Winston Churchill

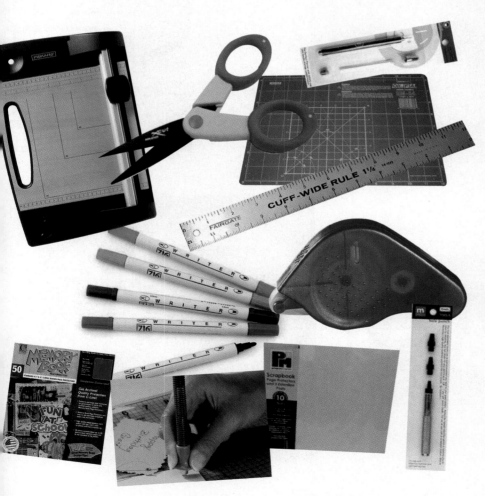

The Tools

TRIMMER
Make large straight cuts quickly and neatly with a 12" trimmer – perfect for paper, photos and cardstock.

SCISSORS
A must-have for any crafter! You need a fine-tipped pair for detailed work and general scissors for trimming and freehand cutting.

ADHESIVES
These include: Glue Dots, liquid glue, 3D foam squares, a Tape Runner, double-sided tape etc. Adhesives must be acid free to ensure your photos remain safe.

SELF-HEALING MAT
This protects both your work surface and your tools when using a craft knife, hole punch, hammer or eyelet setter.

RULER
A 12" metal ruler is necessary for measuring, drawing and for use with a craft knife in straight-line cutting.

PAPER PIERCER
Make small holes through a variety of materials, not just paper! Ideal for using in conjunction with brads, so you don't damage their stems; also good for piercing templates for stitched effects.

HOLE PUNCH
A versatile punch can be used to create holes anywhere on a page, and is especially handy when setting eyelets.

EYELET SETTER
If you plan to use eyelets (metal holed fasteners) on your pages, you will need a specialist setter that splays the backing of the eyelet to attach securely.

PENS
For safe journaling and lettering near photos, use acid-free pigment pens. There are a variety of colours and tip sizes available, so you can be as creative as you like!

PAGE PROTECTORS
Essential for keeping your pages pristine, tucked safely away from sticky fingers and dust.

ALBUM
The hard case for storing and organising finished pages. You can choose from decorated or plain, and post-bound or ring-bound. Albums come in a variety of sizes, colours and materials.

The Extras

CARDSTOCK
The foundation of most page layouts, and available in a massive variety of colours, shades and textures, cardstock is a must-have. Choosing the right one is like deciding on a pair of shoes!

PATTERNED PAPER
Spoilt for choice! Here is where the real fun (and indulgence) begins. There is bound to be one brand you prefer, that suits your style and complements your photos, colour scheme or clothing choice. Be warned! With so much choice, the decision-making process can take a while.

EYELETS & BRADS
These can be used either to attach materials to your page, or as stand-alone accents.

BLOSSOMS & FLOWERS
A fun way to bring a little dimension and frou-frou frill to your layouts. Available in mulberry, silk and paper.

LETTERING
Rub-ons, stickers and monograms are all ideal for quickly adding titles, descriptions, journaling and information. Mix and match for interesting results.

RUBBERSTAMPS
You can safely use your alphabet and image stamps on your page layouts by using an acid-free, archival inkpad.

RIBBON & FIBRE
Soften pages with ribbons and fibres – useful for attaching accents and charms, as well as creating their own focal point.

CHARMS & ACCENTS
Pre-made detailed embellishments add instant impact to page layouts.

SLIDE FRAMES
Slide frames come in paper, plastic and metal and are made specifically to be used with photos. They are acid free and safe for scrapbooks.

TAGS
Perfect for adding dimension and interest to your layout, and they make handy journaling surfaces.

TEMPLATES
A helping hand to get it right first time!

Achievable Scrapbooking

If you have ever had to juggle more than one thing in life, as well as find a moment to squeeze in some 'me' time, this book is for you!

Designed to inspire you to pick up your photos and start creating as well as reach the finish line, we have included some clever solutions for busy scrapbookers to become more effective with your time spent crafting. From time-saving tips to handy gadgets and tools, you will find this resource invaluable in the battle to get that album finished.

I heard once that we can spend five minutes making the memory, and two hours to get it down on a scrapbook layout. It seems like the balance has shifted from living for the moment, to making the moment 'scrap worthy'. Redress the balance and scrap smart. You don't need to skimp on quality, but you do need to follow some simple steps to make your time more effective.

Experts from both sides of 'the Pond' have come together in this book to reveal how they complete projects to a deadline. With a wealth of experience, they share their favourite quick cheats and techniques to ensure results in half the time.

So grab a table and get scrapping... you can do it!

Love

"Happy marriages begin when we marry the ones we love, and they blossom when we love the ones we marry." - Tom Mullen

NOW I KNOW WHAT LOVE IS. —VIRGIL

MUM'S THE WORD
Designer: Debi Potter, Ellison Design

SUPPLIES
Floral paper (DCWV); Cardstock (DCWV); Photo Turn die (Sizzix Originals); Scallop Tag die (Sizzix Originals); Funky Brush & Rat-A-Tat alphabet sets (Sizzix Sizzlits); Window & frame making kit (Sizzix Sizzlits); Simple Impressions Dancing Hearts Background Embossing Folder (Sizzix Sizzlits); Photo corners (Ellison Thin Cuts); Silver metallic card; White vellum; Pink ribbon; Heart die

NOW I KNOW WHAT LOVE IS
Designer: Debi Potter, Ellison Design

SUPPLIES
Beige Rose printed paper (DCWV); Cardstock (DCWV); Vellum Quotes (DCWV); Slide Mount & Coin Holder dies (Sizzix Originals); Rat-A-Tat alphabet set (Sizzix Sizzlits); Window & frame making kit (Sizzix Sizzlits); Photo corners (Ellison Thin Cuts); Silver metallic card; Oyster textured paper; Cream ribbon; Heart die

Album bites

For most people, their wedding is the biggest day of their life... and it makes the perfect starting point for completing an entire album in one weekend. With dozens of cameras focused on the bride and groom as well as all the bridesmaids, flowers and guests, you are assured an abundance of images. Weddings make ideal subjects for scrapbooking as it is easy to pull together images from one theme and event to recreate a seamless walk through the special day. By following some of our designer's tricks and tips, you will be able to complete a beautiful and timeless memento

HOW DO I LOVE THEE?

Designer: Debi Potter, Ellison Design

SUPPLIES

Beige Rose printed paper (DCWV); Beige, dark beige, white & pink cardstock (DCWV); Border Punch strips (DCWV); Photo Turn die (Sizzix Originals); Clock Handles & Buckle dies (Sizzix Originals); Funky Brush & Rat-A-Tat alphabet sets (Sizzix Sizzlits); Window & frame making kit (Sizzix Sizzlits); Photo corners (Ellison Thin Cuts); Bookplates #2 (Ellison Thick Cuts); Silver metallic card; White vellum; Pink ribbon; Pink brad; Heart die

Quick product

When you are creating a layered paper or card background, a quick way to stick down large areas is to use either a spray adhesive or a hand-held dispenser that covers a wide area

Design shortcut

Using more than one font on a layout adds interest, creating more for your eye to take in

LET ME COUNT THE WAYS

Designer: Debi Potter, Ellison Design

SUPPLIES

Beige Rose printed paper (DCWV); Beige, white & pink card (DCWV); Flower set, Tag set & Rat-A-Tat alphabet set (Sizzix Sizzlits); Photo Corners (Ellison Thin Cuts); Silver metallic card; White vellum; Pink ribbon

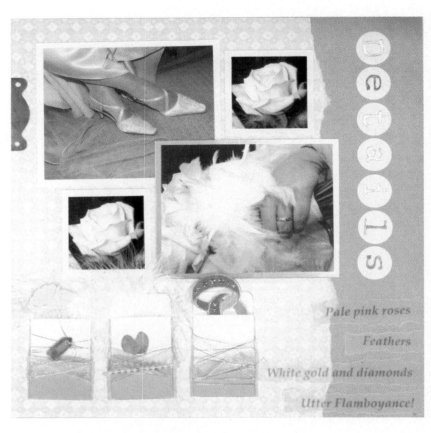

Pale pink roses

Feathers

White gold and diamonds

Utter Flamboyance!

DETAILS

Designer: Debi Potter, Ellison Design

SUPPLIES

Grey printed paper (DCWV); Grey & white card (DCWV); Hinge die (Sizzix Originals); Tag die (Sizzix Sidekick starter pack); Rat-A-Tat alphabet set and Hearts (Sizzix Sizzlits); Silver metallic card; White vellum; Ribbon; Beads; Silver metallic thread

Quick cheat

When decorating a library card holder (see Details layout above) begin by putting a piece of double-sided tape on the back of each one. This will secure the ribbon or thread into position as it is wrapped around

Photo tip

By printing your photos in a range of sizes you will be able to lay them onto your page, giving you more choice when deciding on a layout

GUYS/GIRLS

Designer: Debi Potter, Ellison Design

SUPPLIES

Grey & Pink Text printed papers (DCWV); Grey Diamond & Pink Circular patterned paper (DCWV); White, grey, dark grey & pink card (DCWV); Album & Album Inserts dies (Sizzix Originals); Boxed Brush alphabet set (Sizzix Sizzlits); Simple Impressions Circles Background Embossing Folder (Sizzix Sizzlits); Silver metallic card; Ribbon; Silver thread; Heart die

Design shortcut

Don't waste your scraps of card and paper! Use them in collage backgrounds or as accents

OUR WEDDING DAY
Designer: Debi Potter, Ellison Design

SUPPLIES

Pink Rose, Beige Rose & Pink Circular printed papers (DCWV); Beige card (DCWV); Sticker (DCWV); Photo Turn die (Sizzix Originals); Wedding set, Window & Frame making set (Sizzix Sizzlits); Filmstrip die (Ellison Thick Cuts); Photo Corners (Ellison Thin Cuts); Silver metallic card; Gold textured paper; Ribbon; White vellum; Heart die

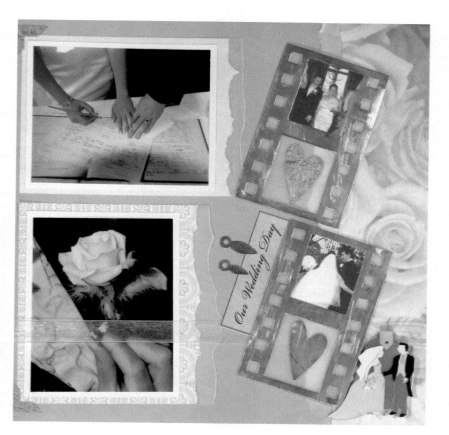

ABOUT TO TIE THE KNOT
Designer: Debi Potter, Ellison Design

SUPPLIES

Pink Text printed paper (DCWV); Pale pink, pink & dark pink card (DCWV); Charms dies (Sizzix Originals); Funky Brush alphabet set (Sizzix Sizzlits); Photo Corners (Ellison Thin Cuts); Circles (Ellison Thick Cuts); Silver metallic card; White vellum; Pink ribbon; Beige brads

The detail

Try using a colour scheme to match that of the wedding and incorporate small keepsakes from the day. You can easily include name settings, invites and other mementoes in the page layouts

Ellison Design Extended Cuts and Sizzix Decorative Strips come in an array of designs and are perfect for scrapbooking with their 12" length, as you can see on the Capture The Moment layout to the right

Design shortcut

Don't be afraid to use black. It often seems to be avoided but can look striking if used in moderation, especially alongside black and white photographs (see the Love Of My Life layout, bottom-right)

MR AND MRS
Designer: Debi Potter, Ellison Design

SUPPLIES
Pink & white card (DCWV); Pink Text printed paper (DCWV); Sticker (DCWV); Funky Brush & Rat-A-Tat alphabet sets (Sizzix Sizzlits); Photo Corners (Ellison Thin Cuts); Silver metallic card

CONFETTI
Designer: Debi Potter, Ellison Design

SUPPLIES
Pink, pale pink & white card (DCWV); Pink Text printed paper (DCWV); Sticker (DCWV); Funky Brush alphabet set & Tag set (Sizzix Sizzlits); Simple Impressions Dancing Hearts Background Embossing Folder (Sizzlits); Window & frame making kit (Sizzlits); Photo Corner (Ellison Thin Cut); Pink ribbon; Silver metallic card; Heart die

Design shortcut

Always die-cut your shape before embossing, as the embossed effect will become damaged if you cut afterwards

CAPTURE THE MOMENT

Designer: Debi Potter, Ellison Design

....

SUPPLIES

Beige Text & Floral printed papers (DCWV); Beige, white & dark beige card (DCWV); Funky Brush & Rat-A-Tat alphabet sets (Sizzix Sizzlits); Window & frame making set (Sizzix Sizzlits); Filmstrip Decorative Strips (Sizzix Sizzlits); Photo Corners (Ellison Thin Cuts); Silver metallic card; Gold textured paper

LOVE OF MY LIFE

Designer: Debi Potter, Ellison Design

....

SUPPLIES

Grey Text & Grey Rose printed paper (DCWV); Grey, black, & white card (DCWV); Printed vellum (DCWV); Hinges die (Sizzix Originals); Scallop Tag die (Ellison Thick Cuts); Photo Corners (Ellison Thin Cuts); Silver metallic card; Silver ribbon; Heart die

Scrapbooking in a weekend REVEALED!

Debi Potter

"I would recommend...

- Writing a list of topics or headings for each page and labelling an envelope for each one. Select the photographs you would like to include in your album and divide them into the appropriate envelopes.

- Keeping to a simple colour scheme. I would advise three neutral shades, one accent colour and a metallic to add interest. Buying a kit like the ones produced by Die Cuts With a View can often work out cheaper and you waste less time worrying about the colours co-ordinating because it is all done for you!

- Working on two pages at a time, like a double page spread in a magazine. It is far easier because an idea for one page can flow onto the next and the overall look of the album will be less disjointed.

- Having all of your supplies at hand before you begin. A trip to the shops will seriously hamper your prospects of completing within a weekend.

- Selecting a workspace within your home that can remain undisturbed throughout the project to save time tidying away and setting up again.

- Ignoring the telephone and locking the doors – only answer the doorbell to the take-away delivery man!"

Album bites

Natalie's mum got married on the Bluebell Railway in Sussex in 2004. Lucky guests were invited to a Civil Ceremony held in the station, which was followed by a reception onboard a travelling steam train. As a gift for her mum, Natalie created an album that captured the day. By cleverly mimicking the pattern and hue of her mum's outfit, she created a stylish co-ordinated album

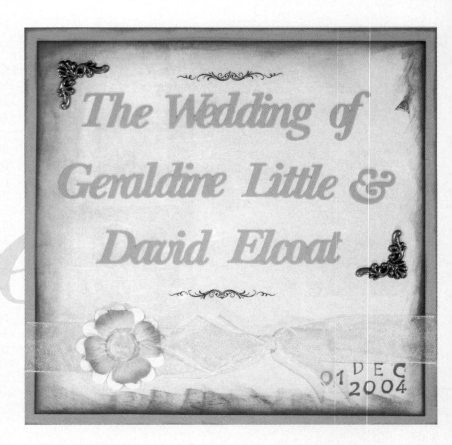

THE WEDDING OF...
Designer: Natalie O'Shea

SUPPLIES

Cardstock (Scrapbook Sally); SweetPea Jack paper (BasicGrey); Rub-ons (7gypsies); Flowers (Prima); Clear button (Hero Arts); Letter stamps (Funstamps); Title (Craft Robo); Photo corners; Black chalk ink; Cream organza ribbon

THE INVITE *Designer: Natalie O'Shea*

SUPPLIES Cardstock (Scrapbook Sally); SweetPea Jack paper (BasicGrey); Rub-ons (7gypsies); Title (Craft Robo); Black chalk ink; Cream organza ribbon; Mulberry paper

GOLDEN ARROW *Designer: Natalie O'Shea*

SUPPLIES Cardstock (Scrapbook Sally); SweetPea Jack paper & tags (BasicGrey); Black chalk ink; Cream organza ribbon

"The goal in marriage is not to think alike, but to think together." — Robert C. Dodds

Design shortcut

Cut circular rub-ons in half and attach to the sides of two adjacent pages to unite a double page spread

JUST WAITING
Designer: Natalie O'Shea

SUPPLIES

Cardstock (Scrapbook Sally); SweetPea Jack paper (BasicGrey); Rub-ons (Jeneva & Co); Titles (Craft Robo); Diamanté gemstones; Black chalk ink

Quick techniques

1 Use a black chalk inkpad to make all the paper edges match the BasicGrey styling and colouring

2 Add diamanté brads to emulate the jewels of the wedding, as in the flowers on page 18

3 Use squares of patterned paper to create patchwork-effect backgrounds

4 Elegant watermark backgrounds can be created by stamping repeatedly with a VersaMark inkpad

5 Include the menu and invite to remember the little details from the day

THE ARRIVAL
Designer: Natalie O'Shea

SUPPLIES

Cardstock (Scrapbook Sally); SweetPea Jack paper (BasicGrey); Rub-ons (Jeneva & Co); Titles (Craft Robo); Diamanté gemstones; Black chalk ink

Adhesive Remover
Dissolvant à colle • Quita pegamento
Easy removal • No smudging
Nettoyage facile • Sans bavure
Fácil de quitar • No mancha

Quick fix

EK Success has a new adhesive remover, so if you put a rub-on in the wrong place you can easily fix it

Design shortcut

Use a big fat lolly stick to apply rub-ons with ease

THE FLOWERS

Designer: Natalie O'Shea

SUPPLIES

Cardstock (Scrapbook Sally); SweetPea Jack Paper (BasicGrey); Metal plaque (Making Memories); Flowers (Prima); Acrylic paint (Ranger); Title (Craft Robo); Black chalk ink

Photo tip

Plan ahead: take close-up photos of the flowers, the ring, and the headdress, as well as group shots and distance shots. That way you will be able to start your album with a varied collection of images

THIS DAY I THEE WED

Designer: Natalie O'Shea

SUPPLIES

Cardstock (Scrapbook Sally); SweetPea Jack Paper (BasicGrey); Blossoms (Making Memories); Rub-ons (Making Memories); Acrylic paint (Ranger); Diamanté brad (Magic Scraps); Black chalk ink

this day i thee wed...

THE REGISTER
Designer: Natalie O'Shea

SUPPLIES
Cardstock (Scrapbook Sally); SweetPea Jack paper (BasicGrey); Metal plaque & frame (Making Memories); Metal words (Making Memories); Title (Craft Robo); Black chalk ink

CELEBRATE
Designer: Natalie O'Shea

SUPPLIES
Cardstock (Scrapbook Sally); SweetPea Jack paper (BasicGrey); Metal words (Making Memories); Fastenator (EK Success); Staples (EK Success); Metal quote plaque (Jo-Ann); Cream organza ribbon; Black chalk ink

Quick tool

Another terrific gadget is the Fastenator from EK Success. It attaches worded staples to any area on your page, adding those finishing touches in no time

Design shortcut

Use the same accent throughout your album (like the organza ribbon) to create a flowing and consistent feel

ETERNAL LOVE
Designer: Natalie O'Shea

SUPPLIES
Cardstock (Scrapbook Sally); SweetPea Jack paper (BasicGrey); Rub-ons (Making Memories); Twill (7gypsies); Metal word (Jo-Ann); Rub-ons (Jeneva & Co); Black chalk ink

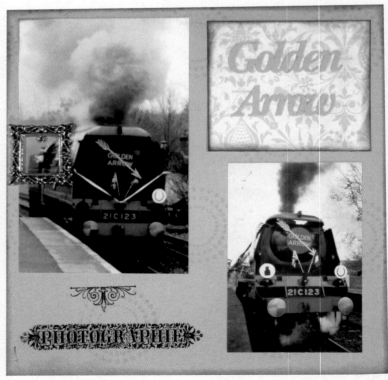

THE BLUEBERRY RAILWAY *Designer: Natalie O'Shea*

SUPPLIES Cardstock (Scrapbook Sally); SweetPea Jack paper (BasicGrey); Rub-ons (7gypsies); Circle Dot stamp (Fontwerks); Inkpad (VersaMark); Title (Craft Robo); Small metal frame; Black chalk ink

HAPPINESS
Designer: Natalie O'Shea

....

SUPPLIES
Cardstock (Scrapbook Sally); SweetPea Jack paper & tag (BasicGrey); Metal key plaque (Making Memories); Rub-ons (Making Memories); Twill (7gypsies); Rub-ons (Jeneva & Co); Metal Groom dot (KI Memories); Bookplate (Go West); Mulberry paper flower; Black chalk ink

A DAY TO REMEMBER
Designer: Natalie O'Shea

....

SUPPLIES
Cardstock (Scrapbook Sally); Rub-ons (7gypsies); Rub-on circle frame (Jeneva & Co); Title (Craft Robo); Black chalk ink

"To save time when scrap-booking, I recommend the following straight-forward steps:

Natalie O'Shea

1. Decide on your album theme.
2. Get together everything that you want to include in your album – the paper, card, embellishments, words and pictures – and lay it all out on the floor or your desk. Stick to this choice.
3. Decide how many pages your want your album to be.
4. Choose which photos you want to go onto which page, crop and print out.
5. Figure out what titles you want to add to each page.
6. Keep it reasonably simple, with the theme running through the whole album. If you only have a few co-ordinated patterned papers and cardstock colours to choose from, the choice is reasonably easy to make.
7. Stick to one colour of embellishments, for example gold or silver.

If you follow the above ideas, you should have no problem in completing an album similar to mine in a weekend. Using an 8x8" size saves time too. By the time you have added a photo or two, you're not left with much more space to embellish. Keep it simple, keep the theme and paper range running throughout and treat each page in a double page spread as a mirror image of the opposite page, so you don't have to think up a new page every time!"

"Love at first sight is easy to understand; it's when two people have been looking at each other for a lifetime that it becomes a miracle." - Amy Bloom

Album bites

There are rarely any photos (after the wedding day) of couples gazing lovingly into each other's eyes! Maybe reality kicks in, and the camera instead becomes focused on family and events. It soon becomes easier to find yourself *behind* the lens than in front of it. So here is the challenge: find some pictures of your spouse and think of all the good things to say about them. Even if it is just a few pages, you may rekindle those newly-wed emotions!

AMORE
Designer: Becks Fagg

SUPPLIES
Cardstock (Prism); Paper (Junkitz); Expressionz rub-ons (Junkitz); Tabz (Junkitz); Wholy Cow! rub-ons (BasicGrey); Adhesive (Woodware); Staples

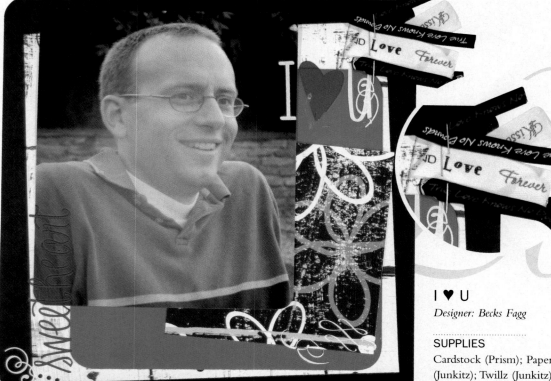

I ♥ U
Designer: Becks Fagg

SUPPLIES
Cardstock (Prism); Paper (Junkitz); Expressionz rub-ons (Junkitz); Twillz (Junkitz); Wholy Cow! rub-ons (BasicGrey); Adhesive (Woodware); Staples

MY WISHES FOR YOU

Designer: Becks Fagg

SUPPLIES

Cardstock (Prism); Paper (Junkitz);
Expressionz rub-ons (Junkitz); Tabz
(Junkitz); Wholy Cow! rub-ons
(BasicGrey); Adhesive
(Woodware); Staples

TONGUES

Designer: Becks Fagg

SUPPLIES

Cardstock (Prism); Paper (Junkitz);
Expressionz rub-ons (Junkitz); Twillz (Junkitz);
Wholy Cow! rub-ons (BasicGrey); Adhesive
(Woodware); Gum Dropz (Junkitz); Staples

Quick fix

The next generation in rub-ons is much slicker and no
longer requires the help of a steamroller to transfer them
onto your project! With designs advancing, rub-ons can
now include delicate detail like these easy-to-use, but
stunningly minute, filigree finish ones.

Design shortcut

If you know how many pages you want in your album, lay everything out on a table and play with the layout to keep each different. Allocate photos before you even open any adhesive!

Quick tip

Staples are a quick way to attach bulky items to your pages, such as ribbon

TOGETHER
Designer: Becks Fagg

SUPPLIES
Cardstock (Prism); Paper (Junkitz); Expressionz rub-ons (Junkitz); Wholy Cow! rub-ons (BasicGrey); Adhesive (Woodware); Staples

HUGS
Designer: Becks Fagg

SUPPLIES
Cardstock (Prism); Paper (Junkitz); Expressionz rub-ons (Junkitz); Wholy Cow! rub-ons (BasicGrey); Adhesive (Woodware); Gum Dropz (Junkitz); Staples

FAMILY
Designer: Becks Fagg

SUPPLIES
Cardstock (Prism);
Paper (Junkitz);
Expressionz rub-ons
(Junkitz); Twillz
(Junkitz); Wholy Cow!
rub-ons (BasicGrey);
Adhesive (Woodware);

MOMENTS LIKE THIS
Designer: Becks Fagg

SUPPLIES
Cardstock (Prism);
Paper (Junkitz);
Expressionz rub-ons
(Junkitz); Gum Dropz
(Junkitz); Wholy Cow!
rub-ons (BasicGrey);
Adhesive (Woodware);
Staples

Scrapbooking in a weekend REVEALED!

"When I want to get an album completed…

Becks Fagg

- I put my photos away and pull out a pen and paper. I love to write, and think of an album as a story in pictures. I first tell the story in writing; jotting down dates, memories, who, where and when. Then when I pull together my photos, they fall into their natural progression and I add them to the pages.

- Getting my kids involved is a mix of time-saving and time-adding! But it is often easier to make the project a family one than to be constantly interrupted by bored little ones. I also find that they add their own versions of events, giving great insights into what really happened in a photo.

- Retreat! Not a cry of surrender, more like a call to arms. If you are adamant about finishing a project, book yourself onto a weekend retreat and hide away from the housework. It makes a refreshing break, is loads of fun and I always throw myself back into the week with added vigour and energy after my 'recharge'.

- Read, read, read… books, magazines, journals and the likes. If I read plenty before I sit down I usually have a mind full of creative ideas. I take some time out to jot my thoughts down and then let the juices flow as I wield scissors and paper."

Die-cutting machines...faq

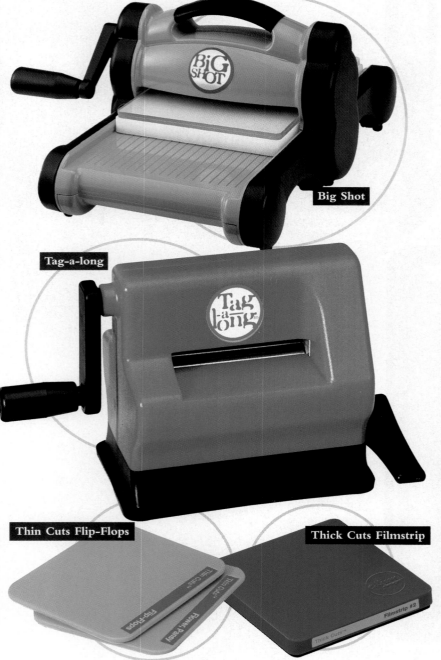

Big Shot

Tag-a-long

Thin Cuts Flip-Flops

Thick Cuts Filmstrip

WHAT IS DIE-CUTTING?

Die-cutting is a technique that has been around for centuries. The term refers to the process of using a machine template to punch holes in, cut out or form shapes from a variety of materials, not dissimilar to using a pastry cutter.

ARE ALL DIE-CUTTING TOOLS ALIKE?

There is a selection of die-cutting tools to choose from. Some are handheld, lightweight, compact and portable, whilst others are bulky but with a multitude of applications beyond paper. Some tools use a rolling mechanism and others act like large pincers, and you must apply pressure manually. Choosing the right tool is usually down to personal preference and what you want to use the machine for.

WHAT MATERIALS CAN I DIE-CUT?

Ellison and Sizzix machines can die-cut, emboss and add textured finishes to many materials including: paper, cardstock, fabric, faux fur, felt, foil, shrink plastic, leather, poly foam, self-adhesive rubber, sheet magnet, sponge, static cling vinyl and thin sheet metal. Not all die-cutting machines are this versatile, however, and most only accommodate paper and card.

HOW DOES DIE-CUTTING SAVE TIME?

Using scissors takes time and patience. Die-cutting transforms the tedious task of trimming intricate letters and shapes into a fast, fun and easy endeavour. You avoid sore fingers and imperfect edges, and you can cut more than one shape at a time, getting projects finished a lot quicker.

....

Check out hundreds of creative ideas online:
www.sizzix.com
www.ellisondesign.com
www.quickutz.com
www.accucut.com
www.spellbinders.us

Childhood

Album bites

Our childhood passes so quickly and is probably one of the most carefree times of our lives. It is full of dreams, imagination, smiles and playful fun. Scrapbooking the memories of our own children somehow reminds me of what it was like to be a kid and may even make it easier to forgive the chocolate smears and pen on the wall!

BABY SOPHIE

Designer: Jenni Bowlin, Li'l Davis Designs

SUPPLIES

Foam Stamps (Li'l Davis Designs); Paint (Li'l Davis Designs); Chipboard word (Li'l Davis Designs); Rhinestone flower (Li'l Davis Designs); Rub-on numbers (Li'l Davis Designs); Frame rubberstamp (Rubber Stampede); Cardstock (Bazzill Basics); Patterned paper (Fontwerks)

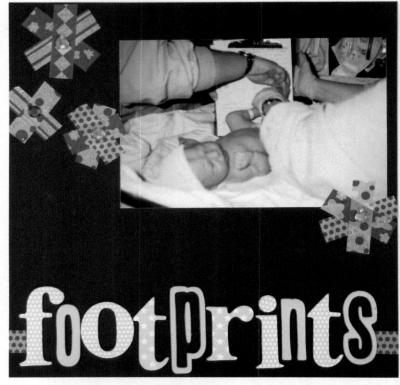

FOOTPRINTS ON MY HEART *Designer: Li'l Davis Design Team*

SUPPLIES Framed & patterned chipboard alphabets (Li'l Davis Designs); Patterned tape (Li'l Davis Designs); Silk flower (Li'l Davis Designs); Architect letter stickers (Li'l Davis Designs); Gems (Making Memories)

> *"People who say they sleep like a baby usually don't have one."* - Leo J. Burke

ME & YOU

Designer: Michelle Baker, Li'l Davis Designs

SUPPLIES

Silk flowers (Li'l Davis Designs); Urban Camo canvas belt & rubber tab (Li'l Davis Designs); Binder clips (Li'l Davis Designs); Ribbon (Li'l Davis Designs); Hollywood patterned papers (Fontwerks)

DREAM

Designer: Michelle Baker, Li'l Davis Designs

SUPPLIES

Silk flowers (Li'l Davis Designs); Urban Camo canvas belt & rubber tab (Li'l Davis Designs); Urban Camo Footnotes (Li'l Davis Designs); Binder clips (Li'l Davis Designs); Ribbon (Li'l Davis Designs); Hollywood patterned papers (Fontwerks)

Quick tips

Apply the oversized Urban Camo Footnote rub-on directly onto the photo, overlapping the edge to create a dramatic title. The definition from the Footnote can be added at a right angle to frame the corner of the photo, drawing the eye to the sleeping baby

Try taking apart the flower embellishments to create clever photo corners, finishing with a simple gem to each centre

LOST IN REVERIE/UNCLE BUB *Designer: Jenni Bowlin, Li'l Davis Designs*

SUPPLIES Footnote & letter rub-ons (Li'l Davis Designs); Letter & label stickers (Li'l Davis Designs); Chipboard flower (Li'l Davis Designs); Ribbon (Li'l Davis Designs); Rhinestone flower (Li'l Davis Designs); Patterned paper (Fontwerks)

Quick trick

Don't be afraid to add rub-ons directly to your photos. They are a great way to dress up an enlarged favourite and are perfect to add a little colour to black and white prints

1ST

Designer: Michelle Hill, Li'l Davis Designs

SUPPLIES

Patterned tape (Li'l Davis Designs); Pink decorative ribbon (Li'l Davis Designs); Pink flower (Li'l Davis Designs); Large book plate (Li'l Davis Designs); Pink safety pin (Li'l Davis Designs); Patterned paper (Fontwerks); Cardstock (Bazzill Basics); Stamping ink (Ranger)

Design shortcut

To create quick and easy custom accents, cut patterned tape into strips in the shape of hearts, arrows and flowers

VISITORS
Designer: Michelle Hill, Li'l Davis Designs

SUPPLIES
Patterned tape (Li'l Davis Designs); Baby Girl binder clips (Li'l Davis Designs); Pink decorative ribbon (Li'l Davis Designs); Vintage wood alphabet & shapes (Li'l Davis Designs); Patterned chipboard alphabet (Li'l Davis Designs); Patterned paper (Fontwerks); Cardstock (Bazzill Basics); Glitter spray paint (Krylon); Stamping ink (Ranger)

You are such a **treasure**

You attended your first church service this morning at our church – Friendship Baptist. You were so

sweet

You slept the entire service on Daddy's lap. You awakened when the service ended – rested, **happy** and ready to babble!

TREASURE *Designer: Faye Morrow Bell, Li'l Davis Designs*

SUPPLIES Ribbon (Li'l Davis Designs); Binder clips (Li'l Davis Designs); Vintage wood words (Li'l Davis Designs); Patterned paper (Fontwerks); Font (Times New Roman); Cardstock (Bazzill Basics); Rhinestone flower (Li'l Davis Designs)

Although Tyler and I spent every single day together,

I always enjoyed the time spent at the changing table.

That was the time that we would CONNECT.

I would share a story or tell her about the project I was working on.

And Tyler ALWAYS had A story of her own to share that she would gleefully babble to me!

TYLER'S STORY *Designer: Faye Morrow Bell, Li'l Davis Designs*

SUPPLIES Flower (Li'l Davis Designs); Ribbon (Li'l Davis Designs); Vintage words (Li'l Davis Designs); Font (Calisto); Cardstock (Bazzill Basics); Patterned paper (Fontwerks); Engineering paper (Staedtler)

Scrapbooking in a weekend REVEALED!

Jenni's tips for creating an album in a weekend:

1. Choose a theme for your album.

2. Choose the photos you'd like to include beforehand, picking out your favourites which truly highlight your theme.

3. Decide on a colour scheme (try three or four colours at most) and organise a pile of papers and embellishments that co-ordinate. This way you will know that everything you reach for will work well together.

4. Make a list of each page theme. For example, in a baby album you would include the newborn's statistics, visitors, first bath, etc. This will help you to move on to each page faster and is a way to be sure that nothing important is left out.

5. Develop a quick list of journaling notes ahead of time. This will keep you from wasting precious moments wondering what to write.

Jenni Bowlin

"There are only two lasting bequests we can hope to give our children. One is roots; the other, wings." — Hodding Carter

DYLAN *Designer: Mandy Anderson*

SUPPLIES

Patterned paper (Pebbles Inc); Market tag (Pebbles Inc); Eyelet brads (Pebbles Inc); Ribbon (Pebbles Inc); Chalk ink (ColorBox); Tag alphabet (Making Memories); Ribbon

Album bites

Albums don't always have to involve big folders and posts. Here Mandy has created an imaginative paper bag album in two easy steps:

1 Lay three paper bags measuring 40x25½cm on top of each other, alternating the open ends.

2 Fold all of the bags in half, crease the edges well and tie them together with string.

MIRACLE

Designer: Mandy Anderson

SUPPLIES

Patterned paper (Pebbles Inc); Market tags (Pebbles Inc); Eyelet brads (Pebbles Inc); Labels (Pebbles Inc); Cardstock (Prism); Chalk ink (ColorBox); Button (Junkitz); Ribbon

Quick cheat

Rather than sewing buttons directly onto a page, thread a button first and then adhere to the page with glue dots, without losing that home-sewn impression

SWEET LITTLE BOY

Designer: Mandy Anderson

SUPPLIES

Patterned paper (Pebbles Inc); Ribbon (Pebbles Inc); Market tag (Pebbles Inc); Candy Dots (Pebbles Inc); Chalk ink (ColorBox)

BABY LOVE

Designer: Mandy Anderson

SUPPLIES

Patterned paper (Pebbles Inc); Ribbon (Pebbles Inc); Square sliders (Pebbles Inc); Eyelet brads (Pebbles Inc); Chalk ink (ColorBox)

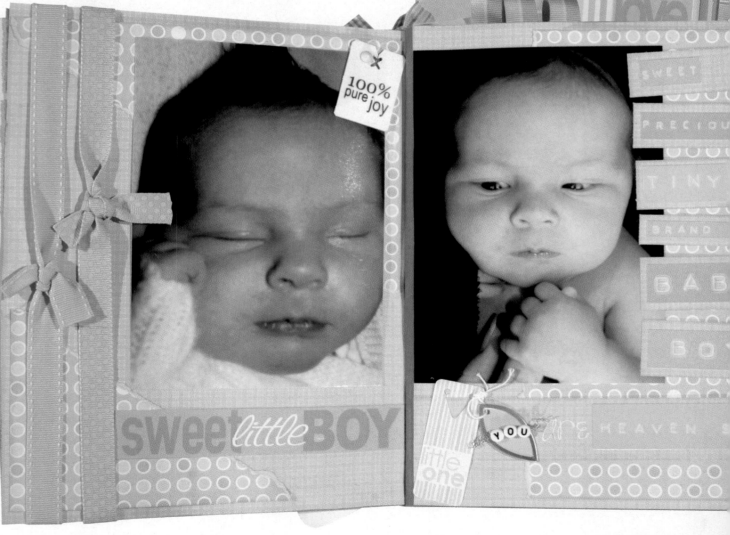

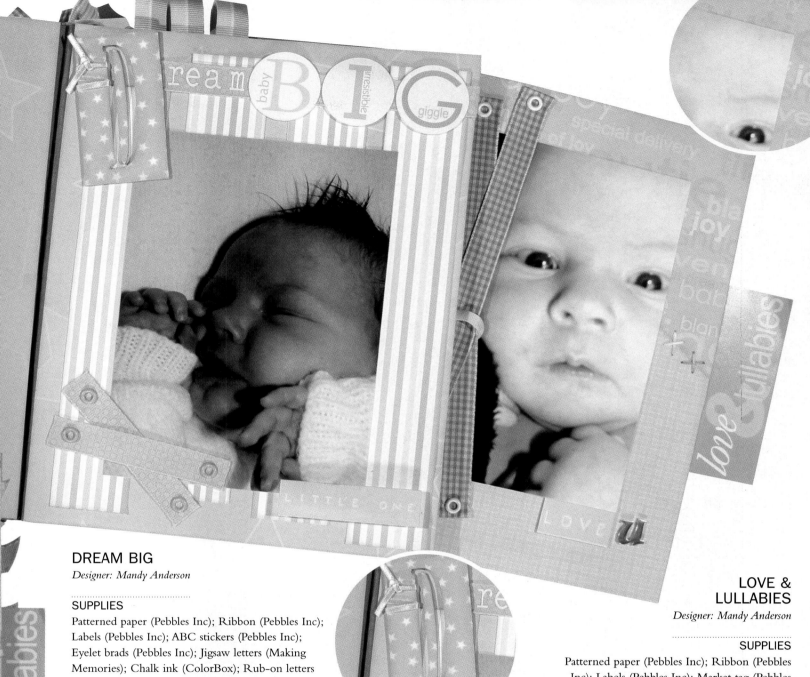

DREAM BIG

Designer: Mandy Anderson

SUPPLIES

Patterned paper (Pebbles Inc); Ribbon (Pebbles Inc); Labels (Pebbles Inc); ABC stickers (Pebbles Inc); Eyelet brads (Pebbles Inc); Jigsaw letters (Making Memories); Chalk ink (ColorBox); Rub-on letters (Gin-X); Ribbon (Gin-X)

LOVE & LULLABIES

Designer: Mandy Anderson

SUPPLIES

Patterned paper (Pebbles Inc); Ribbon (Pebbles Inc); Labels (Pebbles Inc); Market tag (Pebbles Inc); Eyelet brads (Pebbles Inc); Cardstock (Prism); Chalk ink (ColorBox); Scrap metal (Pressed Petals); Embroidery thread

YOU ARE HEAVEN SENT

Designer: Mandy Anderson

SUPPLIES

Patterned paper (Pebbles Inc); Labels (Pebbles Inc); Market tags (Pebbles Inc); Chalk ink (ColorBox); Rub-on alphabet (Making Memories); Buttons (Junkitz); Paper; Metal-rimmed tag; Wire; Embroidery thread

Quick tip

When stapling ribbon onto cardstock, attach it first with glue before stapling to ensure that the ribbon doesn't move when you staple it

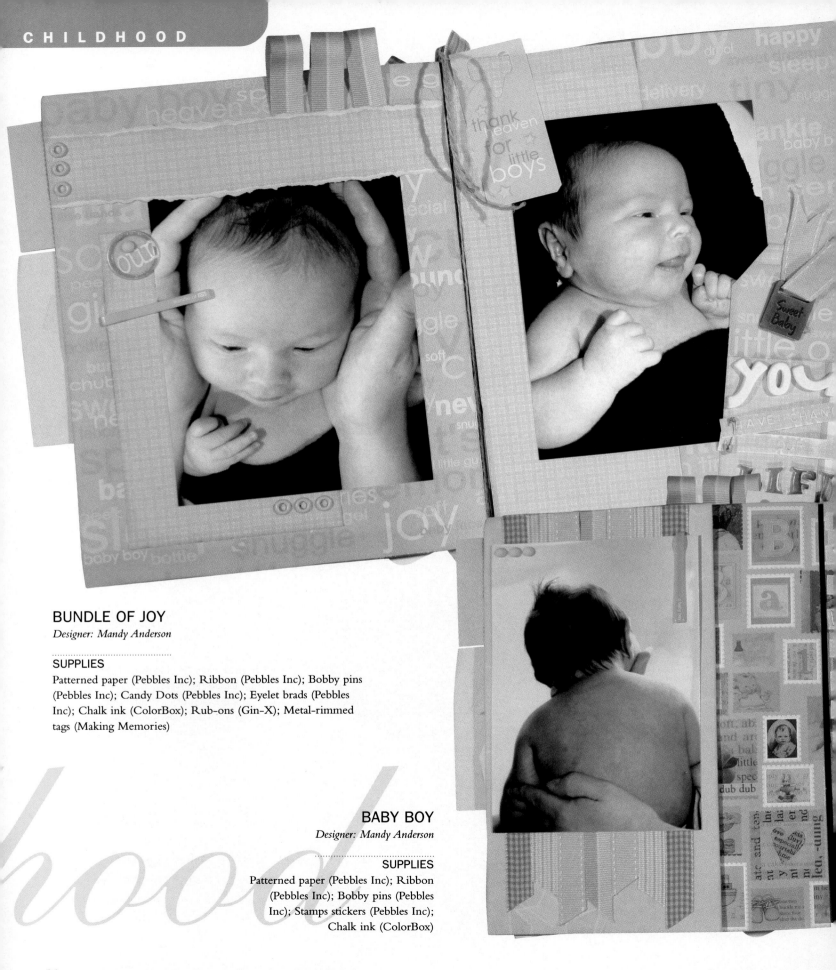

BUNDLE OF JOY

Designer: Mandy Anderson

SUPPLIES

Patterned paper (Pebbles Inc); Ribbon (Pebbles Inc); Bobby pins
(Pebbles Inc); Candy Dots (Pebbles Inc); Eyelet brads (Pebbles
Inc); Chalk ink (ColorBox); Rub-ons (Gin-X); Metal-rimmed
tags (Making Memories)

BABY BOY

Designer: Mandy Anderson

SUPPLIES

Patterned paper (Pebbles Inc); Ribbon
(Pebbles Inc); Bobby pins (Pebbles
Inc); Stamps stickers (Pebbles Inc);
Chalk ink (ColorBox)

SWEET BABY
Designer: Mandy Anderson

SUPPLIES
Patterned paper (Pebbles Inc); Ribbon (Pebbles Inc); Word charms (Pebbles Inc); Market tags (Pebbles Inc); Clay letters (Li'l Davis Designs); Scrap metal (Pressed Petals); Chalk ink (ColorBox); Safety pins (Making Memories); Dymo tape

CHILDREN HOLD
Designer: Mandy Anderson

SUPPLIES
Patterned paper (Pebbles Inc); Ribbon (Pebbles Inc); Word charm (Pebbles Inc); Stamps stickers (Pebbles Inc); Chain (Pebbles Inc); Chalk ink (ColorBox); Dymo tape

Design shortcuts

Create the impression of a long strip of ribbon by attaching small pieces under the top and bottom of a photograph

After you have run strips of patterned paper through a dymo machine, lightly sand or ink the raised surfaces to give the letters definition

Quick cheats

Use a whole sheet of stickers to create an instant background

Masking tape is handy for securing loose ends of ribbon

LITTLE BOY BLUE
Designer: Mandy Anderson

SUPPLIES
Patterned paper (Pebbles Inc); Labels (Pebbles Inc); Square slider (Pebbles Inc); Eyelet brads (Pebbles Inc); Cardstock (Prism); Chalk ink (ColorBox); Scrap metal (Pressed Petals); Rub-ons (Gin-X); Dymo tape

LITTLE FINGERS
Designer: Mandy Anderson

SUPPLIES
Patterned paper (Pebbles Inc); ABC stickers (Pebbles Inc); Labels (Pebbles Inc); Bobby pin (Pebbles Inc); Candy Dots (Pebbles Inc); Chalk ink (ColorBox); Scrap metal (Pressed Petals)

LITTLE TOES
Designer: Mandy Anderson

SUPPLIES
Patterned paper (Pebbles Inc); ABC stickers (Pebbles Inc); Labels (Pebbles Inc); Bobby pin (Pebbles Inc); Candy Dots (Pebbles Inc); Ribbon (Pebbles Inc); Chalk ink (ColorBox)

Scrapbooking in a weekend REVEALED!

"My tips for creating an album in a weekend:

1. Gather together all the photographs you will need to complete the album. Print, resize or do a photo shoot to capture the images you want.

2. Draft an idea of what each page will look like, sketching ideas and journaling that you wish to include.

3. Book yourself a weekend where you can concentrate completely on your album, without distractions.

4. Check your supplies to ensure you don't run out of essentials like glue, cutter blades or ink.

5. Choose a manufacturer and purchase all your supplies from them — co-ordinating paper, cardstock and embellishments will make your job a lot easier."

Mandy Anderson

"I have found the best way to give advice to your children is to find out what they want and then advise them to do it." – Harry S. Truman

Album bites

Collecting memories and scrapbooking about nieces, nephews, friends and cousins can be just as rewarding as filling your album with just your close family. As that age old truth holds, each of us is a sum of the people we have known

BABY GIRL
Designer: Anita MacDonald

SUPPLIES
Patterned paper (BasicGrey); Monograms (BasicGrey); Tags (BasicGrey); Rub-ons (BasicGrey); Fibres (BasicGrey); Notch & Die tool (BasicGrey); Rub-ons (Making Memories)

Quick cheats

Use your chipboard monograms as stencils to use many times over. This will enable you to pick and choose your title colours to co-ordinate with whichever page you are creating

POORLY BABY
Designer: Anita MacDonald

SUPPLIES
Patterned paper (BasicGrey); Monograms (BasicGrey); Tags (BasicGrey); Rub-ons (BasicGrey); Fibres (BasicGrey); Notch & Die tool (BasicGrey); Rub-ons (Making Memories)

CHOCOLATE CAKE
Designer: Anita MacDonald

SUPPLIES
Patterned paper (BasicGrey); Monograms (BasicGrey); Stickers & rub-ons (BasicGrey); Fibres (BasicGrey); Notch & Die tool (BasicGrey);. Undressed Hardware (BasicGrey); Undressed monograms & tags (BasicGrey); Rub-ons (Making Memories); Brads (Making Memories); Flowers (Prima); Ink (Tsukineko)

Quick effect

White-based cardstock and papers lend themselves well to sanding, creating a gentle distressed look around the edges and a more prominent effect. Use fine-grade sandpaper to buff the edges of your papers. Inking paper edges also has this distressing effect

Design idea

Dymo Journaling Cut a thin strip of paper (preferably white cored) and feed it through the Dymo machine. When the journaling is complete, gently sand with fine-grade sandpaper to expose the white core and emphasise the writing. This handy trick enables you to journal onto any colour paper to beautifully co-ordinate with your pages. Alternatively, you could gently buff over card strips with an old inkpad rather than sandpaper, so that the words take the colour of the ink

BLUE EYES
Designer: Anita MacDonald

SUPPLIES
Patterned paper (BasicGrey); Monograms (BasicGrey); Stickers & rub-ons (BasicGrey); Fibres (BasicGrey); Notch & Die tool (BasicGrey); Tags (BasicGrey); Undressed tags (BasicGrey); Brads (Making Memories); Flowers (Prima); Ink (Tsukineko); Dymo tape

Quick trick

Save time: before you adhere your embellishments and photos to the page, move them around until you are completely happy with their placement

SNAILS
Designer: Anita MacDonald

SUPPLIES

Patterned paper (BasicGrey); Monograms (BasicGrey); Stickers & rub-ons (BasicGrey); Notch & Die tool (BasicGrey); Ink (Tsukineko); Letter stickers (Provo Craft)

Quick tool

The BasicGrey Notch & Die cutting tool can be used to make interesting borders and corners to hold both your journaling and photographs or simply to embellish a page. It easily creates closures for mini files, wallets and envelopes and comes with interchangeable heads to create a variety of effects.

TOTALLY POOPED
Designer: Anita MacDonald

SUPPLIES

Patterned paper (BasicGrey); Monograms (BasicGrey); Stickers & rub-ons (BasicGrey); Fibres (BasicGrey); Tags (BasicGrey); Notch & Die tool (BasicGrey); Ink (Tsukineko)

Clever effect

Inkjet transparencies are easy to use and give quick and attractive results for creating a title, some journaling or an overlay to decorate your page

TOOTH FAIRY
Designer: Anita MacDonald

SUPPLIES

Patterned paper (BasicGrey); Monograms (BasicGrey); Rub-ons (BasicGrey); Fibres (BasicGrey); Undressed tags (BasicGrey); Ink (Tsukineko); Brads (Making Memories); Acetate; Inkjet printer; 3D foam squares; Letter stickers

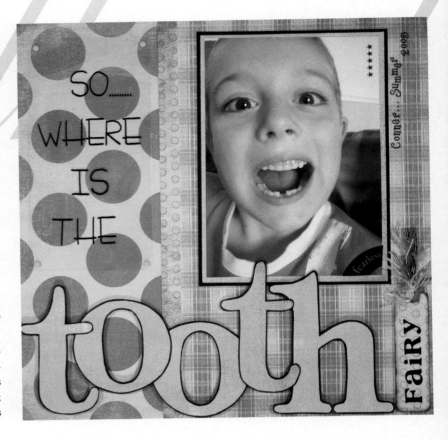

SO........ WHERE IS THE tooth FAiRY

Quick tips

Try using stripy papers in varying directions and widths. This will help to create interesting visual lines, taking only moments to produce

1ST YEAR AT SCHOOL
Designer: Anita MacDonald

SUPPLIES

Patterned paper (BasicGrey); Monogram (BasicGrey); Rub-ons (BasicGrey); Notch & Die tool (BasicGrey); Undressed Hardware (BasicGrey); Ink (Tsukineko)

1ST yeaR @ SCHOOL

Whitehouse Primary 2000

Design shortcut

If you have problems with the colours or patterns in your photograph clashing with your chosen papers, simply change the photo to black and white or sepia tone. This should make it easier to fit your design and can also sometimes enhance the photo by giving it new depth and character

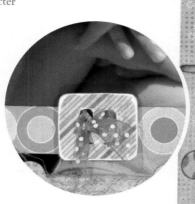

DOWN ON THE FARM
Designer: Anita MacDonald

SUPPLIES

Patterned paper (BasicGrey); Monograms (BasicGrey); Stickers (BasicGrey); Fibres (BasicGrey); Undressed Hardware (BasicGrey); Undressed monograms (BasicGrey); Ink (Tsukineko); Brads (Making Memories); 3D foam squares

MORE THAN JUST SISTERS
Designer: Anita MacDonald

SUPPLIES

Patterned paper (BasicGrey); Monograms (BasicGrey); Stickers & rub-ons (BasicGrey); Fibres (BasicGrey); Notch & Die tool (BasicGrey); Undressed Hardware (BasicGrey); Undressed monograms (BasicGrey); Ink (Tsukineko)

Quick cheats

Use up leftover scraps to make serendipity squares which can be used as embellishments or journaling blocks

To create dimensional monograms, use the undressed monograms as templates to draw round, cut out, ink the edges and then raise onto foam pads. This will give the impression that they are real chipboard ones!

JUST CHILLIN'
Designer: Anita MacDonald

SUPPLIES

Patterned paper (BasicGrey); Stickers (BasicGrey); Rub-ons (BasicGrey); Fibres (BasicGrey); Undressed Hardware (BasicGrey); Notch & Die tool (BasicGrey); Ink (Tsukineko); Brads (Making Memories); Letter stickers (Provo Craft)

Quick trick

If you have extra photos you want to include that don't really fit on the page, try creating a little pocket, file folder booklet or hidden tag to neatly tuck away additional memories and journaling!

Design shortcut

Cut out the shapes from patterned papers to make into embellishments

FIRST LOVE
Designer: Anita MacDonald

SUPPLIES

Patterned paper (BasicGrey); Stickers (BasicGrey); Monograms (BasicGrey); Rub-ons (BasicGrey); Fibres (BasicGrey); Undressed monograms (BasicGrey); Notch & Die tool (BasicGrey); Ink (Tsukineko); Brads (Making Memories); Letter stickers (Provo Craft); 3D foam squares

WAITING FOR SANTA

Designer:
Anita MacDonald

....

SUPPLIES
Patterned paper (BasicGrey); Stickers (BasicGrey); Monograms (BasicGrey); Rub-ons (BasicGrey); Fibres (BasicGrey); Notch & Die tool (BasicGrey); Ink (Tsukineko); Brads (Making Memories); Dymo tape

Scrapbooking in a weekend REVEALED!

"My tips for completing an album in a weekend are:

Anita MacDonald

1. Prepare page kits beforehand, including all the papers, photos and embellishments you would like to use. This will save you from having to scrabble about looking for 'just the right thing'.

2. Create some sketches or plans (see our templates on page 153) for the design of your page – even a basic outline will do, as this will give you a good foundation to start from.

3. Let the papers do the hard work for you. Choose papers that you are happy with and that co-ordinate and complement each other – they will be much easier to work with.

4. Create quick titles or journaling by making good use of monograms, rub-on letters and transparencies.

5. Above all, if you relax and enjoy it, the rest will just fall into place."

YOU ARE SNOW SPECIAL

Designer: Anita MacDonald

....

SUPPLIES
Patterned paper (BasicGrey); Stickers (BasicGrey); Monograms (BasicGrey); Rub-ons (BasicGrey); Fibres (BasicGrey); Undressed tag (BasicGrey); Notch & Die tool (BasicGrey); Ink (Tsukineko); Letter stickers (Provo Craft)

"There is nothing like a newborn baby to renew your spirit and to buttress your resolve to make the world a better place." -Virginia Kelley

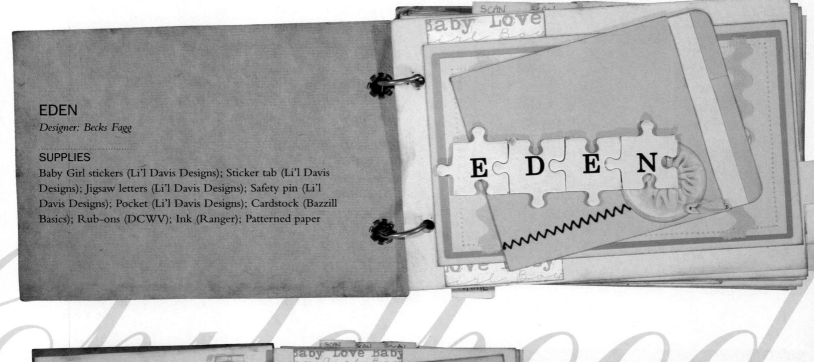

EDEN

Designer: Becks Fagg

SUPPLIES

Baby Girl stickers (Li'l Davis Designs); Sticker tab (Li'l Davis Designs); Jigsaw letters (Li'l Davis Designs); Safety pin (Li'l Davis Designs); Pocket (Li'l Davis Designs); Cardstock (Bazzill Basics); Rub-ons (DCWV); Ink (Ranger); Patterned paper

A: THE BEGINNING

Designer: Becks Fagg

SUPPLIES Sticker tab (Li'l Davis Designs); Jigsaw letters (Li'l Davis Designs); Cardstock (Bazzill Basics); Plain paper (Pebbles Inc); Ink (Ranger); Patterned paper

B: WONDER

Designer: Becks Fagg

SUPPLIES Sticker tab (Li'l Davis Designs); Jigsaw letters (Li'l Davis Designs); Epoxy sticker (Li'l Davis Designs); Cardstock (Bazzill Basics); Plain paper (Pebbles Inc); Ink (Ranger); Patterned paper

C: BUNDLE OF JOY
Designer: Becks Fagg

SUPPLIES
Epoxy sticker (Li'l Davis Designs); Jigsaw letters (Li'l Davis Designs); Safety pin (Li'l Davis Designs); Cardstock (Bazzill Basics); Ink (Ranger); Patterned paper

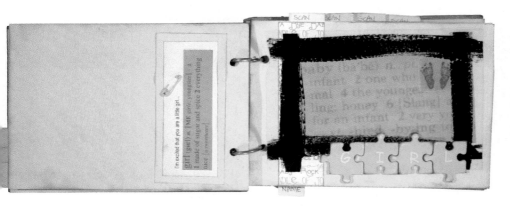

GIRL
Designer: Becks Fagg

SUPPLIES Transparency (Li'l Davis Designs); Sticker tab (Li'l Davis Designs); Jigsaw letters (Li'l Davis Designs); Safety pin (Li'l Davis Designs); Cardstock (Bazzill Basics); Plain paper (Pebbles Inc); Ink (Ranger); Patterned paper

MY SCAN PHOTOS 1
Designer: Becks Fagg

SUPPLIES Transparency (Li'l Davis Designs); Sticker tab (Li'l Davis Designs); Jigsaw letters (Li'l Davis Designs); Safety pin (Li'l Davis Designs); Pocket (Li'l Davis Designs); Baby Girl sticker (Li'l Davis Designs); Cardstock (Bazzill Basics); Plain paper (Pebbles Inc); Ink (Ranger); Patterned paper

Quick tips

Using pre-made embellishments like layered stickers saves you time while giving your project a dimensional feel

Big titles make bold headlines and instantly grab the attention of the reader

Design shortcut

If your album does not have page protectors, use easy-to-access pockets and flaps to conceal photos you want to keep from being handled

INNOCENCE 2
Designer: Becks Fagg

SUPPLIES

Transparency (Li'l Davis Designs); Sticker tab (Li'l Davis Designs); Jigsaw letters (Li'l Davis Designs); Safety pin (Li'l Davis Designs); Pocket (Li'l Davis Designs); Baby Girl sticker (Li'l Davis Designs); Epoxy sticker (Li'l Davis Designs); Cardstock (Bazzill Basics); Plain paper (Pebbles Inc); Ink (Ranger); Patterned paper

Quick cheat

If you don't want to pull out all your ink and stamps, try using transparencies. The ones used here look like stamped images, but without the mess!

Quick fix

If you struggle to fix transparencies to your project without the adhesive showing, position an embellishment or photo over it to hide the adhesive behind

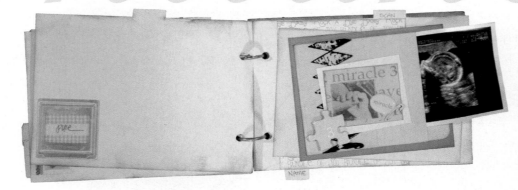

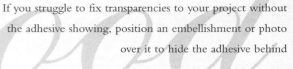

MIRACLE 3
Designer: Becks Fagg

SUPPLIES

Transparency (Li'l Davis Designs); Sticker tab (Li'l Davis Designs); Jigsaw letters (Li'l Davis Designs); Safety pin (Li'l Davis Designs); Pocket (Li'l Davis Designs); Baby Girl sticker (Li'l Davis Designs); Epoxy sticker (Li'l Davis Designs); Cardstock (Bazzill Basics); Plain paper (Pebbles Inc); Ink (Ranger); Patterned paper

GIVING YOU A NAME...
Designer: Becks Fagg

SUPPLIES

Sticker tab (Li'l Davis Designs); Jigsaw letters (Li'l Davis Designs); Cardstock (Bazzill Basics); Ink (Ranger); Patterned paper

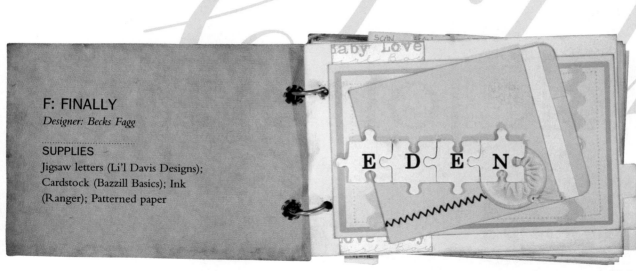

F: FINALLY

Designer: Becks Fagg

SUPPLIES

Jigsaw letters (Li'l Davis Designs);
Cardstock (Bazzill Basics); Ink
(Ranger); Patterned paper

Design shortcut

Use fibres to fill any empty space on a page, adding texture to your album

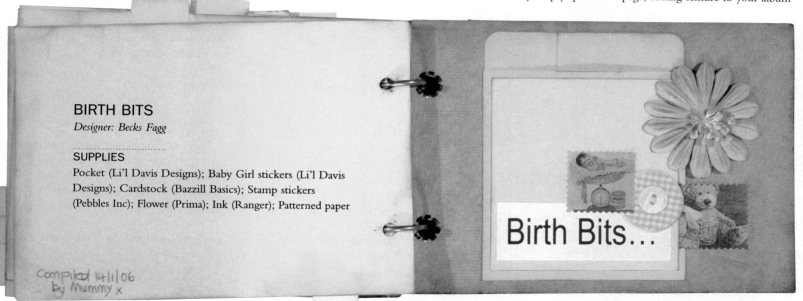

BIRTH BITS

Designer: Becks Fagg

SUPPLIES

Pocket (Li'l Davis Designs); Baby Girl stickers (Li'l Davis
Designs); Cardstock (Bazzill Basics); Stamp stickers
(Pebbles Inc); Flower (Prima); Ink (Ranger); Patterned paper

Scrapbooking in a weekend REVEALED!

"To use your time for scrapbooking effectively:

Get organised! One of the biggest drains on your time is not knowing where all your supplies are located, and not having them within easy reach! Being organised takes a little time to start with, but you will become a more effective scrapbooker and your creativity will benefit as a result.

Define your space Define your work space and have everything located (and labelled) close by. Not all of us have the luxury of craft rooms or tables allocated specifically for our hobby (thank goodness for the kitchen table), but if you at least have a small cupboard or a rolling tote or even a dark corner for boxes, your space can be used to really improve your time spent scrapbooking.

You will find starting off with these basics will make a real difference to your scrapbooking: with everything to hand and ready for use, when you find yourself with 30 minutess to spare, you won't spend 20 minutes digging around for that piece of paper you know you bought last week!"

Becks Fagg

Quick journaling

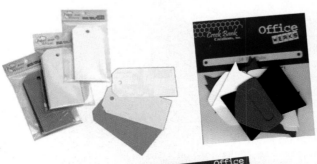

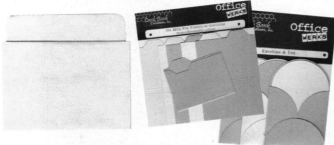

Words add meaning. You can't sing a song without them, it's just a melody. A scrapbook is equally empty without journaling – it may as well be just a picture book

Whether you have a million and one things to say, or you are the strong silent type, by including some form of journaling you will leave a little piece of yourself on each page, ensuring the story gets told and adding meaning beyond the pictures.

Here are some quick cheats for adding journaling to your pages...

HIDDEN TREASURE
We don't always want to bare our soul to everyone and his neighbour, so hiding your writing can be an important element of journaling. It means we can share thoughts without reservation.

Hidden journaling also adds more space to your layout, as you don't have to worry about fitting in the words and can concentrate on the design.

WHERE TO HIDE
Use tags, pockets, mini file folders, tabs, notes tucked behind photos, envelopes and flaps.

JOURNALER'S BLOCK
Occasionally we all get tongue-tied, so try a few of these tips to kick-start the ink flow.

THE BASICS
Answer the who, what, where, when and why of your photo.

Try including a Q&A sheet. Ask the subject of the photo or layout to lend a hand, answering questions on their favourite things, top tens, hobbies etc.

BEYOND THE BASICS
A good place to start is with a pen and paper. Think about the memory of a person, character traits, what you remember about why you took the photo, and what you most want people to know about it. If you imagine you're writing a letter to your children or to a close friend, you will find your journaling will be more personal, and 'sound' like you!

PENMANSHIP
It is something wonderful to find an old letter from a friend or a loved one, as their handwriting conveys their personality just as much as the words they wrote. Including your own handwriting in your scrapbooking is important, as it tells a small part of the story too.

It isn't cheating to use a computer! If you have plenty to say, a computer is a superb tool to condense writing while keeping it legible.

Either way, writing is all about the words, so try and get them down – hidden or on show; handwritten or typed!

"A picture, it is said, is worth a thousand words, but cannot a few well-spoken words convey as many pictures?" – Author Unknown

Birthdays

"When I approach a child, he inspires in me two sentiments — tenderness for what he is, and respect for what he may become." - Louis Pasteur

Album bites

Sometimes it's easier to collect layouts from selected friends and family to quickly compile a varied overview of your theme. The idea is similar to a 'share book' or circle journal, and forms a clever album in an instant!

Here the team have created a celebration of birthdays, and like children, no one page is the same!

1 BIG MESS

Designer: Marla Kress, BasicGrey

SUPPLIES

Blitzen paper & monograms (BasicGrey); Undressed monograms (BasicGrey); Blitzen tags & letter stickers (BasicGrey); Card (Bazzill Basics); Georgia font

JULIA

Designer: Theresa Lundström, BasicGrey

SUPPLIES

Patterned paper (BasicGrey); Undressed monograms (BasicGrey); Chipboard Hardware (BasicGrey); Lucky letter stickers & Wholy Cow! rub-ons (BasicGrey); Got Flowers? (Prima); Deckle-edged scissors (Fiskars); Folk Heart punch (EK Success); CK font; Ink; Chalk; Brads; Lace; Thread; Metal Deco corner

Quick tip

Try using your monogram letters with ink, or mount them to really make them appear like they're popping out of the page

Quick inspiration

Why not look through women's magazines, or at adverts on the TV and on billboards, for creative ways to lay out your pages. Opening titles and credits on TV programmes are also a great place to find inspiration – just have a pen and paper handy!

FUN 2 B
Designer: Becky Fleck, BasicGrey

SUPPLIES
Colour Me Silly paper & letter stickers (BasicGrey); Undressed Hardware & monograms (BasicGrey); Cardstock (Bazzill Basics); Ribbon (American Crafts); Hole punch

Quick tip

Tearing, as opposed to cutting, rags and ribbon will give them a distressed look

REVIEW OF 2
Designer: Marla Kress, BasicGrey

SUPPLIES
Fusion paper & letter stickers (BasicGrey); Cardstock (Bazzill Basics); Georgia & Quigley fonts

HAPPY BIRTHDAY
Designer: Kelly Goree, BasicGrey

SUPPLIES
Colour Me Silly paper (BasicGrey); Chipboard Hardware & tags (BasicGrey); Alpha stickers (Heidi Swapp); 3D sticker (Provo Craft); Rickrack (Doodlebug Design); Ink (ColorBox); Brads (Jest Charming); Buttons (Dress It Up); Pen (Zig)

ABC *Quick tool*

Your computer can become your best friend in scrapbooking, as it is a source of infinite fonts. Try searching online for new fonts (there are loads of free download sites) and really mix it up

Quick tip

Use numbers or lists to quick-start journaling or title ideas

Photo tip

When taking a photo of someone, focus on their eyes – the result will 'speak' volumes!

WISH
Designer: Marla Kress, BasicGrey

SUPPLIES
Vagabond paper & letter stickers (BasicGrey); Undressed monograms (BasicGrey); Cardstock (Bazzill Basics); Georgia & LHF Sofia fonts

TURNING THREE

Designer: Becky Fleck, BasicGrey

SUPPLIES

Oh Baby! Girl paper (BasicGrey); Oh Baby! Boy letter stickers (BasicGrey); Deco scissors (Provo Craft); Got Flowers? (Prima); Broadsheet font; Hand-cut frame

Photo tips

Moving closer to the subject of your photo will give you better results. Try and fill the lense with their face for a real impact shot

If your photos clash with the paper you want to use, get them printed in black and white – then they will go with anything

Quick make

Back one piece of patterned paper with card; doodle a frame shape on the back and cut out with a craft knife. Run journaling around the outside of the matted photo. From the bottom-right corner of the frame, lightly trace a swirl pattern in pencil and cover with punched flowers and mulberry flowers

CANDLES & CAKE

Designer: Kelly Goree, BasicGrey

SUPPLIES

Skate Shoppe paper (BasicGrey); Chipboard Hardware (BasicGrey); Letter stickers (BasicGrey); Cardstock (Bazzill Basics); Ink (ColorBox); Pen (Zig); Computer fonts

YOU'RE INVITED
Designer: Marla Kress, BasicGrey

....

SUPPLIES

Skate Shoppe paper & letter stickers (BasicGrey);
Cardstock (Bazzill Basics); Georgia & Scriptorium fonts

Design shortcut

Create an instant memory montage by grouping photos together

Quick tip

To add texture, try adding ribbon, wool, rickrack, cord or fabric
strips. You can sew them on or use a quick staple

THE KNIGHT CAKE
Designer: Theresa Lundström, BasicGrey

....

SUPPLIES

Fusion paper, tags & fibres (BasicGrey); Undressed
monograms (BasicGrey); Chipboard Hardware
(BasicGrey); Chalk Ink (ColorBox); Vellum; Brads;
Ribbon

Quick tip

Don't forget the detail! Writing between the lines – or
even writing, full stop – will add more interest to your
pages, and also makes them more meaningful

YOUR SPECIAL DAY
Designer: Becky Fleck, BasicGrey

....

SUPPLIES

Oh Baby! Girl paper & letter stickers (BasicGrey);
Cardstock (Bazzill Basics); Hole punch; Persimmon font

Quick make

Cut out four 'candles' from scraps of different patterned paper. Sketch
a candle flame and cut the number 4 from another paper design. Tuck
the candles behind the '4' circle

Quick tool

Use the Notch & Die tool to create
scallop edges, and then lightly sand to
give definition

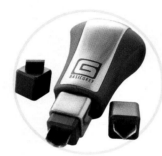

TURNING FOUR
Designer: Kelly Goree, BasicGrey

....

SUPPLIES

Phresh & Phunky paper (BasicGrey); Chipboard
Hardware (BasicGrey); Notch & Die tool
(BasicGrey); Cardstock & brads (Bazzill Basics);
Acrylic paint (Plaid); Ribbon (Offray); Floss (DMC);
Pen (Zig); Ink (ColorBox)

Quick tip

....

Hand-paint chipboard elements to match the papers

FIVE FINGERS – FIVE YEARS
Designer: Theresa Lundström, BasicGrey

SUPPLIES
Black Tie paper & letter stickers (BasicGrey); Lollipop Shoppe paper & letter stickers (BasicGrey); Notch & Die tool (BasicGrey); Deckle-edged scissors (Fiskars); Chalk ink (ColorBox); Kunstler Script font; Brads; Thread; Buttons; Lace

BIRTHDAY WISHES
Designer: Kelly Goree, BasicGrey

SUPPLIES
Paper, letter stickers & Chipboard Hardware (BasicGrey); Cardstock (Bazzill Basics); Floss (DMC); Ink (ColorBox); Pen (Zig); Pen (Uniball)

Quick tips

Try creating your own accents in advance

Recycle and re-use embellishments and accents from cards, or even use the cards in your layout design

6 CANDLES

Designer: Theresa Lundström, BasicGrey

SUPPLIES

Alyssa paper, letter stickers & tags (BasicGrey); Sublime paper & tags (BasicGrey); Notch & Die tool (BasicGrey); Got Flowers? (Prima); Ink (ColorBox); Amazone font; Lace; Brads; Ribbons

Julias 6:e födelsedag!
Det firade vi bl.a med att bjuda in
Medlekompisarna till barnkalas
Övriga små fingrar öppnade fina presenter
sedan bjöd vi på Anki-tårta
med mycket grädde och
näbb & fötter av mandelmassa,
mycket populärt!
5 februari 2005

Scrapbooking in a weekend REVEALED!

Theresa Lundström

Here are Becky's 5 tips for creating a quick album...

1. Select a small group of patterned papers and embellishments to use throughout the album.

2. Create a page sketch and rotate it 90 degrees for each page.

3. Print all photos the same size for consistency.

4. Select two fonts: one for journaling and one for titles. Keep the point size consistent page to page. (Titles work well at 18pt and journaling at 10 or 12, depending on the size of the album.)

5. If photos are from different time periods and some do not match well with the choice of patterned papers, try converting all photos to black and white or sepia.

Quick tip

To create a weathered look on the edge of the patterned paper, I roughed up the edges of the paper with sandpaper

"Our birthdays are feathers in the broad wing of time." - Jean Paul Richter

When I turned three my Mum made me my cake, I loved the Mr Men, and Mr happy was my favourite. The picture was taken outside the flat that we lived in. I loved my red sandals.

Aug '80

LITTLE PRINCESS

THREE
Designer: Michelle Grant

SUPPLIES
Paper, rub-ons & charms (All My Memories); Cardstock (Bazzill Basics); Printed journaling

SIX
Designer: Michelle Grant

SUPPLIES
Charm, Goodie brads & rub-ons (All My Memories); Cardstock (Bazzill Basics); Flowers (Prima); Ribbon

Album bites

Sometimes simple is all it needs to get the job done! Over-fussing isn't for everyone, and the idea behind this album is one you can easily copy. Use photos taken at each yearly landmark, and chart the growing up advents. You can add to the album and watch it build!

1 CHINESE RESTAURANT
2 GREEDY EYES
4 COURSES
ONE 7 YEAR OLD

SEVEN
Designer: Michelle Grant

SUPPLIES
Paper, Goodie brads, rub-ons & charms (All My Memories); Cardstock (Bazzill Basics); Distress ink & Cut n' Dry foam (Ranger); Dymo

My mum made me a white dress,
Not red or pink or blue.
She said it was a special dress
Like very other few.
There has been just one before,
A dress now put away,
That I wore some time ago
Upon my blessing day.
As a little baby clothed
In my first white dress,
My dad held me in his arms,
There to name and bless.
So pure and clean was I just then,
With time to grow and learn
About the Father's plan for me.
My glory I must earn.
Now I've reached the age to judge
The wrong road from the right,
And I am here to be baptized
In this dress of white.
So once again I'm free from sin.
The path is clear to me.
I'll grasp the rod and hold on tight,
I vow with certainty.
Just as mud would stain my dress,
Sin would stain my soul.
The key is to repent or bleach,
For whiteness is my goal.
And if I try my very best,
Then richly blessed I'll be,
Wearing inside God's holy house
White dress number three.
So today I make this pledge:
I'll strive to choose the right,
Through this sacred baptism ordinance
In my second dress of white.

EIGHT *Designer: Michelle Grant*

SUPPLIES Ribbons, rub-ons & charms (All My Memories);
Cardstock (Bazzill Basics); Distress ink, Cut n' Dry foam
(Ranger); Dymo; Vellum

Quick tip

Stick with one manufacturer – products are designed to work together, so why
make life more difficult than you need to by trying to find co-ordinating items?

Scrapbooking in a weekend REVEALED!

"To get a project finished I recommend...

1. Go with a theme. This will help you to select your photos and the products for your album more easily.

2. If you want to create a project super quick, choose a small format album (this one is a 6x6"). This way you will lose less materials and also the smaller pages come together quicker.

3. Hide your journaling – you will be limited for space with the smaller page size, so don't cut out the journaling, just hide it.

4. Who, where and when – you may know this information but will your children or grandchildren if you don't record it?

5. Use your own writing – it is easier and often neater to use a PC and print out your journaling, but your own handwriting will become a much-loved treasure in years to come.

6. Prepare a space before you start, and make sure that everything is sorted and collected together for the album. This will make the whole project so much speedier. I collect themed or related items together in zip-lock bags along with notes of who, where, when, and any specific memories that I would like to include. This creates a 'ready-to-scrap' kit for when I have the time to sit down."

Michelle Grant

Time-saving products

Pre-cut monograms

Die-cut tags

Co-ordinating ranges

Rub-ons

Overlays

Stack packs

AMM page kits

So you finally find yourself with a free hour in the day. You've decided that the ironing mountain will remain unconquered, and the dishes can wait... now is *your* time to craft!

Don't waste the moment – use some of these clever page solutions for quick fixes and finishes, and find yourself completing a layout easily in under an hour!

PRE-CUT MONOGRAMS

Ideal for an instant title or a big attention-grabber. Try using the first letter of the subject's name.

DIE-CUT TAGS

No messing with scissors here – a die-cut tag makes an instant journaling template that can co-ordinate with your background paper and layout design.

CO-ORDINATING RANGES

Having these to hand can mean you have everything prepared and saves digging around in your craft stash for that final accent.

RUB-ONS

A quick-fix alternative to adding embellishments, handwritten details and stamped effects.

OVERLAYS

The finishing touch to photos and background paper, for a simple yet elegant page! Cut them up or use whole... the decision will take longer than the layout!

STACK PACKS

Have a huge array of patterned and plain paper and cardstock all at your fingertips, co-ordinating and ready to cut.

AMM PAGE KITS

A pre-designed layout – just add photos and trimmings for a perfect time-saving solution.

Home & Family

"Families are like fudge.

JANUARY
Designer: Stacey Panassidi

SUPPLIES
Paperz (Junkitz); Epoxy Stickerz (Junkitz);
Labelz & numbers (Junkitz); Cardstock
(Bazzill Basics)

FEBRUARY
Designer: Janna Wilson

SUPPLIES
Paperz (Junkitz); Twillz (Junkitz); Labelz &
date/list (Junkitz); Fabric Button (Junkitz)

JULY

Designer: Stacey Panassidi

....

SUPPLIES

Paperz (Junkitz); Labelz (Junkitz);
Plaid Swatchz (Junkitz); Jump Ringz
(Junkitz); License Platez (Junkitz);
Cardstock (Bazzill Basics)

Quick stick

....

Need a different way to stick and adhere embellishments to your pages?
Try using: • brads, eyelets or nailheads • acid-free spray glue • vellum
tape • sewing • staples • double-sided acid-free tape • glue dots
• ribbon • Xyron machine

AUGUST

Designer:
Janna Wilson

....

SUPPLIES

Paperz (Junkitz); Labelz
(Junkitz); Twillz
(Junkitz); Collectionz
Buttonz (Junkitz)

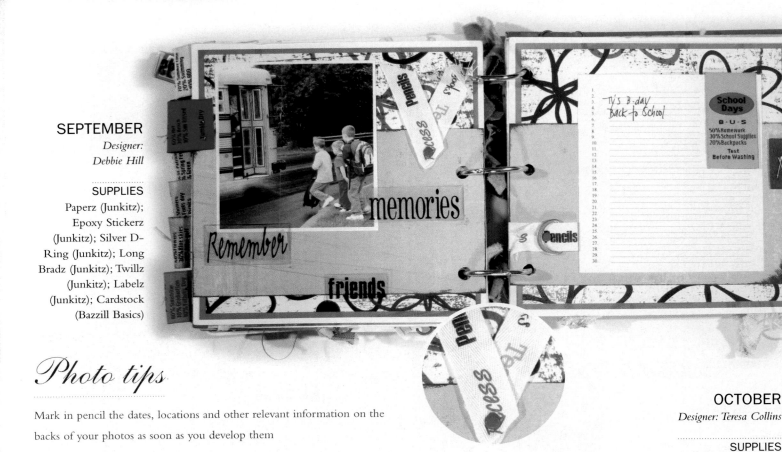

SEPTEMBER

Designer:
Debbie Hill

....

SUPPLIES

Paperz (Junkitz);
Epoxy Stickerz
(Junkitz); Silver D-
Ring (Junkitz); Long
Bradz (Junkitz); Twillz
(Junkitz); Labelz
(Junkitz); Cardstock
(Bazzill Basics)

Photo tips

Mark in pencil the dates, locations and other relevant information on the backs of your photos as soon as you develop them

Save money by ordering copies of photos when you get them developed

OCTOBER

Designer: Teresa Collins

....

SUPPLIES

Paperz (Junkitz); Matz (Junkitz); Swatchz (Junkitz); Binderz (Junkitz); Labelz (Junkitz)

NOVEMBER
Designer: Annette Lauts

SUPPLIES
Paperz (Junkitz); Buttonz (Junkitz); Labelz (Junkitz); Long Bradz (Junkitz); Tim Holtz Wire Pinz (Junkitz); Cardstock (Bazzill Basics)

DECEMBER
Designer: Candice Cook

SUPPLIES
Paperz (Junkitz); Twillz & Twill Snapz (Junkitz); Labelz & Gum Dropz (Junkitz); Long Bradz (Junkitz); Expressionz (Junkitz); Buttonz (Junkitz); Paper Clipz (Junkitz)

Scrapbooking in a weekend REVEALED!

Theresa's top tips for creating quick albums:

"**1.** I make sure my photos all co-ordinate – whether by theme, location or by event. It makes them easier to work with when they go well together.

2. I try to use the same colour combinations. It means I don't have to recreate a page afresh each time, and can repeat certain key elements to ensure the album has a flow and rhythm.

3. When creating my album I always think about what accents I want to use. I use the same ones regularly to build a continuous identity and feeling. If I like a ribbon it will then feature on a couple of my pages, pulling it all together.

4. Limit bulkiness! I really think hard about not over-embellishing, as I want my album to close.

5. I love to include hidden journaling. It tells the story within the album, which is important. I use tags, mini file folders and notes tucked behind my photos. It's a clever way to get extra room, and not have all your darkest secrets on show!"

Teresa Collins

"You don't choose your family. They are God's gift to you, as you are to them." – Desmond Tutu

TIMELESS LOVE
Designer: Kimberley Kesti, Daisy D's

SUPPLIES
Paper & card (Daisy D's); Alphabet stickers (Daisy D's); Decorative brad (Making Memories); Ribbon (May Arts); Journaling pen; Photo turns; Bookplate

Album bites

Heritage is more than just 'old stuff', it's a matter of where we come from, and a great deal of who we are. Celebrating the past in our scrapbooks is as important as celebrating today and tomorrow.

This album spans the decades and comes full circle from our grandparents' wedding days to our own, from children to their flying from the nest. It is a story that rarely gets told all in one place, and is therefore a great place to start!

A GLIMPSE OF HEAVEN
Designer: Kellene Truby, Daisy D's

SUPPLIES
Patterned paper & card (Daisy D's); Hinge (Daisy D's); Ribbon; Alphabet stickers

50 YEARS

Designer: Nena Earl, Daisy D's

....

SUPPLIES

Patterned paper & card (Daisy D's); Attic Heirloom
tab (Daisy D's); Metal hinges (Daisy D's)

Quick make

....

Vintage and aged doesn't always mean 'old', and it's easy to antique or
distress brand new paper with some quick techniques:

Try spraying water on the paper (away from your photos!) and then
crumpling and flattening it several times. Allow it to dry, glue onto
chipboard frames or embellishments and press down. The wrinkles in the
paper are then perfect for rubbing ink over gently, creating a worn
appearance without the wear and tear!

LOVE

Designer: Daisy D's Design Team

....

SUPPLIES

Attic Heirloom patterned paper (Daisy D's); Attic Heirloom
alphabet stickers (Daisy D's); Attic Heirloom flowers (Daisy
D's); Bookplate, hinge & copper photo corners (Daisy D's)

Quick tool

A straight edge ruler is a perfect tool for lining up photos, matts etc

A DREAM COME TRUE
Designer: Kellene Truby, Daisy D's

SUPPLIES
Patterned paper & card (Daisy D's); Hinge (Daisy D's); Coin holder (Daisy D's); Alphabet stickers & sentiments (Daisy D's)

MARRIAGE
Designer: Daisy D's Design Team

SUPPLIES
Patterned paper & card (Daisy D's); Bookplate & copper photo corners (Daisy D's); Attic Heirloom flower (Daisy D's); Transparency (Daisy D's);

Quick bits

Bookplates are great for titling or adding a date or message on your layout

Transparencies are easy to use as there is no messy stamping involved – but you still get the great effect!

YOU ARE MY...
Designer: Nena Earl, Daisy D's

SUPPLIES
Patterned paper & card (Daisy D's); Attic Heirloom alphabet & sentiments stickers (Daisy D's); Distress ink (Ranger); Chipboard alphabet (Making Memories); Vintage buttons

Designer tip

Water down paint and sweep across a colour wash on the patterned paper to soften the colours and mute the vivacity

20 YEARS
Designer: Kimberley Kesti, Daisy D's

SUPPLIES
Paper & card (Daisy D's); Attic Heirloom tags (Daisy D's); Attic Heirloom letters & sentiments stickers (Daisy D's); Ribbon

The future

Sometimes it is important to also look ahead – dream a little on paper! Children soon grow up, and the story comes full circle. Writing down your hopes and dreams for them can be just as interesting to look back on when they are married with their own children

THE KEYS TO MY HEART

Designer: Natasha Roe, Daisy D's

SUPPLIES

Patterned paper & card (Daisy D's); Attic Heirloom tags (Daisy D's); Copper photo corners (Daisy D's); Attic Heirloom alphabet stickers (Daisy D's); Ribbon; Charm; Sewing machine

WE ADORE YOU

Designer: Nena Earl, Daisy D's

SUPPLIES

Patterned paper (Daisy D's); Hinges (Daisy D's); Card (Bazzill); Rub-ons (Chatterbox); Paper flowers (Prima); Paint; Staples; Silk ribbon

Design tips

* Use a variety of items to attach your tags, including: decorative brads, buttons, ribbons or staples
* Use machine stitching to give a finished look to the edges of photo matts
* Avoid a cluttered look by layering tags on tags

YOU CAPTURED MY HEART *Designer: Kellene Truby, Daisy D's*

SUPPLIES Patterned paper & card (Daisy D's); Copper photo corners (Daisy D's); Attic Heirloom sentiments stickers (Daisy D's); Sewing machine

You Captured MY heart

Quade & Korie - Summer

2004

Design team tips for time-saving scrapbooking:

1. Gather your photos ahead of time. Print sizes you like and convert some to black and white to mix things up a little bit. This adds variety and interest to your album.

2. Create a small notebook ahead of time filled with family stories, traditions, etc. This will give you great journaling prompts. You could also put some of your favourite quotes in the notebook.

3. Pack yourself a little lunch and have your favourite snacks on hand. You won't have to think what to eat!

4. Gather your three favourite idea books for when you run out of inspiration.

5. Send the family camping for the weekend!

6. Limit your colour schemes so that you stay focused.

7. Have copies already made of your photos.

"The reason grandparents and grandchildre

GRANDPARENTS: GOD'S GIFT TO CHILDREN

Designer: Anne Hafermann

SUPPLIES

Paper (Daisy D's); Attic Heirloom patterned paper & cardstock (Daisy D's); Attic Heirloom alphabet stickers & sentiments (Daisy D's); Attic Heirloom flower (Daisy D's); Scrapbook adhesive tabs (3L); My Muse, Arizona & AL Charisma fonts (2Peas)

DEDICATION PAGE

Designer: Anne Hafermann

SUPPLIES

Attic Heirloom patterned paper & cardstock (Daisy D's); Attic Heirloom alphabet stickers, sentiments & tags (Daisy D's); Attic Heirloom coin holder (Daisy D's); Attic Heirloom flower (Daisy D's); Scrapbook adhesive tabs (3L); My Muse, Arizona & AL Charisma fonts (2Peas); Transparency

Album bites

The relationship between grandparent and grandchild is one of pure indulgence!

TABLE OF CONTENTS *Designer: Anne Hafermann*

SUPPLIES Attic Heirloom patterned paper & cardstock (Daisy D's); Attic Heirloom flowers (Daisy D's); Attic Heirloom photo corners (Daisy D's); Scrapbook adhesive tabs (3L); My Muse, Arizona & AL Charisma fonts (2Peas); Vellum; Transparency

GENEROUS
RELIABLE
ATTENTIVE
NURTURING
DEDICAT

GENEROUS

Designer: Anne Hafermann

SUPPLIES

Attic Heirloom patterned paper & cardstock (Daisy D's); Attic Heirloom alphabet stickers (Daisy D's); Scrapbook adhesive tabs (3L); My Muse, Arizona & AL Charisma fonts (2Peas); Vellum

RELIABLE

Designer: Anne Hafermann

SUPPLIES

Attic Heirloom patterned paper & cardstock (Daisy D's); Attic Heirloom alphabet stickers & sentiments (Daisy D's); Scrapbook adhesive tabs (3L); My Muse, Arizona & AL Charisma fonts (2Peas); Vellum

ATTENTIVE

Designer: Anne Hafermann

SUPPLIES

Attic Heirloom patterned paper & cardstock (Daisy D's); Attic Heirloom alphabet stickers & sentiments (Daisy D's); Scrapbook adhesive tabs (3L); My Muse, Arizona & AL Charisma fonts (2Peas); Vellum

NURTURING
Designer: Anne Hafermann

SUPPLIES

Attic Heirloom patterned paper & cardstock (Daisy D's); Attic Heirloom alphabet stickers & sentiments (Daisy D's); Attic Heirloom flower (Daisy D's); Scrapbook adhesive tabs (3L); My Muse, Arizona & AL Charisma fonts (2Peas); Vellum

DEDICATED
Designer: Anne Hafermann

SUPPLIES

Attic Heirloom patterned paper & cardstock (Daisy D's); Attic Heirloom alphabet stickers (Daisy D's); Attic Heirloom flower (Daisy D's); Scrapbook adhesive tabs (3L); My Muse, Arizona & AL Charisma fonts (2Peas); Vellum

PATIENT
Designer: Anne Hafermann

SUPPLIES

Attic Heirloom patterned paper & cardstock (Daisy D's); Attic Heirloom alphabet stickers (Daisy D's); Attic Heirloom coin holder (Daisy D's); Scrapbook adhesive tabs (3L); My Muse, Arizona & AL Charisma fonts (2Peas); Vellum

ADDICTIVE *Designer: Anne Hafermann*

SUPPLIES Attic Heirloom patterned paper & cardstock (Daisy D's); Attic Heirloom alphabet stickers (Daisy D's); Scrapbook adhesive tabs (3L); My Muse, Arizona & AL Charisma fonts (2Peas); Vellum

YOUR FAVOURITE KEEPSAKES

Designer: Anne Hafermann

SUPPLIES
Attic Heirloom patterned paper & cardstock (Daisy D's); Attic Heirloom alphabet stickers & sentiments (Daisy D's); Attic Heirloom flower (Daisy D's); Scrapbook adhesive tabs (3L); My Muse, Arizona & AL Charisma fonts (2Peas)

Scrapbooking in a weekend REVEALED!

Anne's tips:

Anne Hafermann

"1. Choose a single layout design and use it on all your pages. You can individualise pages (if desired) with photos, journaling and embellishments, but you will save loads of time and achieve an album with a good flow if you stick with a single basic layout.

2. Use kits or co-ordinating products from one line or manufacturer. I used to feel this took away some of the fun, as I enjoy playing with and combining different products, but it takes up loads of time.

3. Work in stages; cut all your papers in one stage, assemble and adhere background papers for all pages at one time, crop and cut all photos together, do all your journaling at one time, etc. This will save a tremendous amount of time and allow you to completely clean up from one task before moving onto the next. With this method you won't complete any one full page until the very end, but the end will come sooner if you are organised and efficient in this way.

4. Print all your photos before you even begin your project.

5. For a quick and effective way to add journaling, add your words to vellum or acetate and adhere using vellum tape.

6. Take frequent, short breaks and have lots of your favourite snacks and drinks readily available!"

Scrapbooking A-Z

Acetate A form of acidic plastic that causes photos, paper and documents to deteriorate and fade over time.

Acid free Materials that have a pH balance of 7.0 or higher. Many papers are considered acid free straight from the press. However, unless they have been buffered (treated with a neutralising agent), chemical reactions with substances such as when sizing or bleaching will cause the paper to become acidic over time. All plastic by its nature is acid free; however some plastic is unsafe for use in photo albums.

Adhesives The glue used to attach and secure photographs and other components onto a scrapbook page. Adhesive types include photo corners (clear plastic stick-on or paper lick-and-stick style) which are considered non-permanent; and photo tape, photo tabs and tape runner (all forms of double-sided tape), which are considered permanent and photo safe.

Album A blank book used to store scrapbooking photographs and pages.

Archival Term to describe a product or technique used in preserving artefacts, photographs and memorabilia.

Blocking When two materials stick together unintentionally. For instance, a photograph sticking to the back of the next page.

BOM Abbreviation for Book of Me – a scrapbook of any size focusing on details and events, interests and achievements all about the author.

Bone folder A tool used to impress a fine line or crease onto a piece of paper or cardstock to make folding much easier and neater. Although called bone folders, they can also be made out of plastic.

Border The margins of a scrapbook page, usually spoken of in terms of decoration.

Brads Similar to everyday office split pins, but found in many different sizes, shapes and colours. Commonly used for embellishments.

Buttons Available in many different shapes, styles and colours. There are also many buttons that are made specifically for scrapbooking. They tend to be flat and can be attached with fibres, thread or glue.

Cardstock Sturdy paper, available in a variety of weights for scrapbooking.

Chalk Not regular children's chalk, this is specially designed to be safe for scrapbooking and similar paper arts.

Clipart Small images purchased in book or software form that can easily be applied to scrapbooking pages.

Collage An artistic composition made using various materials (paper, cloth, wood etc) that are glued onto a surface.

Colour wheel A wheel-shaped graphic image that shows colour relationships and placement.

Corner-edged scissors Scissors that cut corners. Each pair creates four different types of corners.

Corrugated paper Thick, wavy cardstock available in many colours.

Crop A term used for a gathering of scrapbookers who congregate to work on their albums and page layouts. A crop can also be a formally hosted event with an expert who shares techniques, products and information with the group.

Crop/cropping To cut or trim a photograph in order to highlight a certain area, cut out unwanted activity, or simply to change the photograph's shape.

Dauber A round miniature stamp pad which is dabbed onto a stamp to apply ink.

Decorative ruler A normal ruler with a special edge used in designing scrapbook pages.

Decorative scissors Scissors with a decorative pattern on the blade, to cut patterned edges.

Die-cuts Paper designs and shapes cut using dies.

Double-mount To place a photo on two background papers.

Dry brushing Applying chalk or paint to a brush or sponge and removing most of it by dabbing it on a piece of paper before using it. This prevents the paint from bleeding under the edges of a stencil and the chalk from looking too dark.

Dry embossing/debossing To make a raised image by pushing the paper up with the aid of a stylus from the reverse. Also known as blind embossing.

Embellishment Any scrapbooking supply that enhances the pages, such as brads, eyelets, fibres and charms.

Emboss To create a raised design on paper – either by heating embossing powder on a stamped image, or by using a stylus to trace a brass embossing template.

Embossing ink A glycerin-based ink used for embossing.

Embossing powder Powder sprinkled, usually on stamped images, and heated to create raised edges.

Eyelet A round metal embellishment with a hole in the centre, set by punching a hole and hammering down the back.

Fibre A decorative thread used to adorn scrapbook pages.

Focal point The element of a design where the eye is naturally drawn.

Font The style of lettering. Many fonts can be downloaded free from the internet.

Gel-based rollers Pens with pigment ink.

Handmade paper Paper made by hand that is often rough and uneven in texture. Sometimes there are flowers and leaves in the paper which can add a natural look to your scrapbook.

Hand-tinting (also photo-tinting) A method of applying colour to a black and white photograph.

Heading The caption or title that explains the theme of a layout.

Heat gun Also known as a thermal or embossing gun. A hobby tool that produces heat, but not air. It's used primarily to emboss.

Heritage Traditions passed down from generation to generation.

Hermafix/Herma A brand of dispensing tool for photo-mounting squares.

Hinge album A plastic strap binding that allows your albums to expand. These tend to lay flatter than post-bound albums.

Idea books Books usually about one aspect of scrapbooking. Some are written for particular scrapbooking themes (weddings, babies etc) while others are devoted to a particular scrapbook product (stickers, die-cuts or templates, for example).

Journaling The words you write in your scrapbook. This can include captions, detailed descriptions, poems or stories.

Journaling templates Templates with space left specifically for writing.

Turn to page 156 to continue the run through scrapbooking terms

"*Women and cats will do as they please, and*

Album bites

We humans have had a long-lasting love affair with our pets! We dote on the little critters, and treat them as one of the family. So it makes sense to give them their own scrapbook album

PUPPY LOVE

Designer: Sue Roberts

SUPPLIES

Roundabout, Brushed Box & Serif alphabets (Ellison Design); Die-cuts (Sizzix Sizzlits); Paper & cardstock (DCWV); Tabs (DCWV); Alpha stickers (DCWV)

MAX *Designer: Sue Roberts*

SUPPLIES Roundabout, Brushed Box & Serif alphabets (Ellison Design); Die-cuts (Sizzix Sizzlits); Paper & cardstock (DCWV); Tabs (DCWV); Alpha & Ribbon stickers (DCWV)

Sit

Bella & Lola

best buds

Design shortcut

Download a Dymo-styled font to use if you don't have a Dymo machine

BELLA & LOLA
Designer: Sue Roberts

SUPPLIES
Roundabout, Brushed Box & Serif alphabets (Ellison Design); Die-cuts (Sizzix Sizzlits); Paper & cardstock (DCWV); Tabs (DCWV); Alpha & Ribbon stickers (DCWV)

Photo tips

Get in the picture! Sometimes it's easier to stand behind the camera, but remember to hand it over to someone else occasionally

Scan in all your pictures before you start, this way they are ready to print out at the size you require when you are ready for them

LOLA
Designer: Sue Roberts

SUPPLIES
Roundabout, Brushed Box & Serif alphabets (Ellison Design); Die-cuts (Sizzix Sizzlits); Paper & cardstock (DCWV); Tabs (DCWV); Alpha & Ribbon stickers (DCWV)

Lola

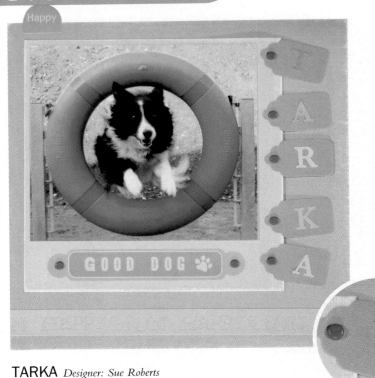

TARKA *Designer: Sue Roberts*

SUPPLIES Roundabout, Brushed Box & Serif alphabets (Ellison Design); Die-cuts (Sizzix Sizzlits); Paper & cardstock (DCWV); Tabs (DCWV); Alpha stickers (DCWV)

LET SLEEPING DOGS LIE *Designer: Sue Roberts*

SUPPLIES Roundabout, Brushed Box & Serif alphabets (Ellison Design); Die-cuts (Sizzix Sizzlits); Paper & cardstock (DCWV); Tabs (DCWV); Alpha stickers (DCWV)

CUTE & FURRY *Designer: Sue Roberts*

SUPPLIES Roundabout, Brushed Box & Serif alphabets (Ellison Design); Die-cuts (Sizzix Sizzlits); Paper & cardstock (DCWV); Tabs (DCWV); Alpha & Ribbon stickers (DCWV)

PADDY COOL
Designer: Sue Roberts

SUPPLIES

Roundabout, Brushed Box & Serif alphabets
(Ellison Design); Die-cuts (Sizzix Sizzlits);
Paper & cardstock (DCWV); Tabs (DCWV);
Alpha & Ribbon stickers (DCWV)

FOREVER A COMPANION
Designer: Sue Roberts

SUPPLIES

Roundabout, Brushed Box & Serif
alphabets (Ellison Design); Die-cuts
(Sizzix Sizzlits); Paper & cardstock
(DCWV); Tabs (DCWV); Alpha
stickers (DCWV)

Quick tip

Bend the perforations on your Sizzlits
dies and attach to the layout with
foam pads to give a 3D feel

Design shortcut

Use the outer piece of the die-cut
as a stencil and create your own
background by inking dog paw prints
across your paper

PUPPY EYES
Designer: Sue Roberts

SUPPLIES

Roundabout, Brushed Box & Serif
alphabets (Ellison Design); Paper &
cardstock (DCWV)

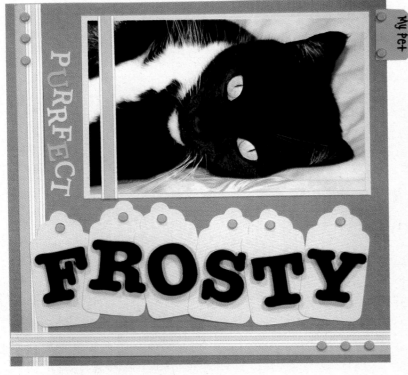

FROSTY

Designer: Sue Roberts

SUPPLIES

Roundabout, Brushed Box & Serif alphabets (Ellison Design); Die-cuts (Sizzix Sizzlits); Paper & cardstock (DCWV); Tabs (DCWV); Alpha & Ribbon stickers (DCWV)

FLUFFY

Designer: Sue Roberts

SUPPLIES

Roundabout, Brushed Box & Serif alphabets (Ellison Design); Die-cuts (Sizzix Sizzlits); Paper & cardstock (DCWV); Tabs (DCWV); Alpha & Ribbon stickers (DCWV)

SABRE

Designer: Sue Roberts

SUPPLIES

Roundabout, Brushed Box & Serif alphabets (Ellison Design); Die-cuts (Sizzix Sizzlits); Paper & cardstock (DCWV); Tabs (DCWV); Alpha & Ribbon stickers (DCWV)

Quick tools

- Die-cutting machine
- Sizzix Sidekick
- Paper trimmer
- Foam pads
- Herma tab dispenser

MY LITTLE GIRL
Designer: Sue Roberts

....

SUPPLIES
Roundabout, Brushed Box & Serif alphabets (Ellison Design); Die-cuts (Sizzix Sizzlits); Paper & cardstock (DCWV); Tabs (DCWV); Alpha stickers (DCWV); Brads

Scrapbooking in a weekend REVEALED!

"My secrets for creating quickly:

1. Keep the pages simple.
2. Mount all your photographs onto cardstock at the same time.
3. The DCWV Scrapbook Kit in a Stack is excellent because it has all the cardstock, patterned papers, stickers, alphabets and quotes you need, so you spend less time trying to match papers and more time scrapping.
4. Bullet-point your journaling.
5. Scrap double layouts and mirror the left-hand side with the right-hand side. You could always rotate the design if you want a bit more variety, as I have done on my Cute & Furry layout."

Sue Roberts

RANDALL'S FARM
Designer: Sue Roberts

....

SUPPLIES
Roundabout, Brushed Box & Serif alphabets (Ellison Design); Die-cuts (Sizzix Sizzlits); Paper & cardstock (DCWV); Tabs (DCWV); Alpha stickers (DCWV)

Internet Resources

The internet makes our lives easier, and if we can fight our way past our offspring and spouse, then we are sure to find a wealth of crafty knowledge at our fingertips. So if you find yourself with a mouse and a spare moment, check out some of these great websites for scrapbookers...

Information

Need to find out how, why, what and where? Find out here:

SCRAPDIRECTORY

www.scrapdirectory.co.uk

Everything under one roof specifically for the UK scrapbooker - shops, forums, events, reviews and more

TOP 50 SCRAPPERS

www.top50scrappers.co.uk

Lists the top scrapbooking-related sites based in the UK

SCRAPBOOKING TOP 50 SITES

www.scrapbookingtop50.com

Lists the top 50 scrapbooking-related sites worldwide

Digital scrapbooking

The busy scrapbooker's solution – find out how with help from these sites:

SCRAP GIRLS

http://scrapgirls.com

DIGITAL SCRAPBOOK PLACE

www.digitalscrapbookplace.com

SCRAPBOOK BYTES

www.scrapbook-bytes.com

Online digital photo developing

Photo developing has never been so easy in this digital age...

PHOTOBOX	SNAPFISH	TRUPRINT
www.photobox.com	www.snapfish.com	www.truprint.co.uk

Forums

If you like to chat, you will love the community of fellow scrapbookers you will find at these forums:

UKSCRAPPERS

www.ukscrappers.co.uk

The leading UK-based scrapbooking forum with galleries, beginner's guides, a library of links, challenges, contests, and frequent 'cybercrops'

TWO PEAS IN A BUCKET

www.twopeasinabucket.com

Worldwide community of scrapbookers, based in the US

THE LOUNGE AT BUMBLE BEE CRAFTS

www.bumblebeecrafts.net

Tips, advice and inspiration shared between scrappers

SCRAPBOOK STASHERS

www.scrapbook stashers.com

General chat about scrapbook-related topics, plus links and resources, a comedy corner and inspirational poems and quotes

Best Friends

Friendship

"Shared laughter creates a bond of friendship. When people laugh together, they cease to be young and old, teacher and pupil, worker and boss. They become a single group of human beings." – W. Lee Grant

FOREVER FRIENDS

Designer: Mandi Coombs, All My Memories

SUPPLIES

Paper (All My Memories); Ribbon (All My Memories); Brad (All My Memories); Rub-ons & sticker (All My Memories); Stencil phrase (All My Memories); Cardstock (Bazzill Basics)

THE BETTER PART...

Designer: Mandi Coombs, All My Memories

SUPPLIES

Paper (All My Memories); Ribbon (All My Memories); Brads (All My Memories); Rub-ons (All My Memories); Stencil phrase (All My Memories); Cardstock (Bazzill Basics)

BEST FRIENDS

Designer: Mandi Coombs, All My Memories

SUPPLIES

Paper (All My Memories); Brads (All My Memories); Crystal ribbon slide (All My Memories); Cardstock (Bazzill Basics)

GIRLFRIENDS

Designer: Mandi Coombs, All My Memories

SUPPLIES

Paper (All My Memories); Sticky Little Words (All My Memories); Brads (All My Memories); Cardstock (Bazzill Basics)

THE BEST OF FRIENDS

Designer: Mandi Coombs, All My Memories

SUPPLIES

Paper (All My Memories); Sticky Little Words (All My Memories); Brads (All My Memories); Accent bar (All My Memories); Cardstock (Bazzill Basics)

KNOWS EXACTLY

Designer: Mandi Coombs, All My Memories

SUPPLIES

Paper (All My Memories); Ribbon (All My Memories); Charm (All My Memories); Jump rings (All My Memories); Rub-ons (All My Memories); Sticker (All My Memories); Guitar pick (All My Memories); Cardstock (Bazzill Basics)

BEST FRIENDS
Designer: Mandi Coombs, All My Memories

SUPPLIES
Paper (All My Memories); Charms (All My Memories); Brads (All My Memories); Rub-ons (All My Memories); Sticker (All My Memories); Daisy accents (All My Memories); Cardstock (Bazzill Basics)

Quick tip

Sign up to online newsletters to receive regular email shots full of ideas and inspiration to keep you motivated

Check out **www.twopeasinabucket.com** or **www.scraptutor.com**

IT'S A GIRL THING
Designer: Mandi Coombs, All My Memories

SUPPLIES
Paper (All My Memories); Charm (All My Memories); Sticky Little Words (All My Memories); Brads (All My Memories); Cardstock (Bazzill Basics)

BIG THINGS
Designer: Mandi Coombs, All My Memories

SUPPLIES
Paper (All My Memories); Sticky Little Words (All My Memories); Brads (All My Memories); Rub-ons (All My Memories); Daisy accents (All My Memories); Cardstock (Bazzill Basics)

SWEETNESS OF FRIENDSHIP

Designer: Mandi Coombs,
All My Memories

SUPPLIES

Paper (All My Memories); Brads
(All My Memories); Rub-ons
(All My Memories); Cardstock
(Bazzill Basics)

TOGETHER

Designer: Mandi Coombs,
All My Memories

SUPPLIES

Paper (All My Memories); Daisy
accents (All My Memories); Cardstock
(Bazzill Basics)

Quick tip

If you struggle with journaling, try having an 'interview' with the person in
the photo and get their input

Quick tip

Mix and blend fonts on your
page by using different letters
of the alphabet (stamps,
stickers or die-cuts) in one
word or title

MY FRIEND

Designer: Mandi Coombs, All My Memories

SUPPLIES

Paper (All My Memories); Sticky Little
Words (All My Memories); Brads (All My
Memories); Guitar picks (All My
Memories); Cardstock (Bazzill Basics)

Scrapbooking in a weekend REVEALED!

Mandi's tips:

Mandi Coombs

"1. **Have a plan, choose your tools, and make a list.** Make all the important decisions about format and organisation first: what type of album, its style and size, whether you will organise it chronologically or by theme. Decide on a colour scheme and pick out the paper, ink, etc as well as your decorative accents. Decide what tools you will use (trimmer, scissors, eyelet setters, chalk, ink, etc) and compile swatches of your chosen colours.

2. **Compile.** Once you've decided what products to use, gather together what you have, and head to your local scrapbook store to get the rest. Collect together all of your photos and memorabilia that you want to use.

3. **Organise.** Organise the photos and memorabilia into the order that they need to be scrapped. Make one pile for each page you are planning. You'll find it easier to keep track of your photos and it will keep you focused on the page you are currently working on.

4. **Keep it clean.** After you complete each page, re-organise your area. Throw away the small scraps and organise the big ones. Re-organise your tools. This gives you a chance to regroup and will allow you to start over with each page. It will also help you keep track of those small tools that always manage to get lost in the endless piles of scraps! You will save time if you're not searching for the same pen over and over again.

5. **Save your list.** If you are creating an album that can be added to in the future, keep your list and swatches so that when the time comes to add to it, you'll have a quick reference sheet for gathering your supplies together again."

THE BEST THINGS
Designer:
Mandi Coombs,
All My Memories

....

SUPPLIES
Paper (All My Memories); Ribbon (All My Memories); Rub-ons (All My Memories); Stickers (All My Memories); Cardstock (Bazzill Basics)

DESTINY'S SISTERS
Designer:
Mandi Coombs,
All My Memories

....

SUPPLIES
Paper (All My Memories); Rub-ons (All My Memories); Sticker (All My Memories); Cardstock (Bazzill Basics)

BEST FRIENDS
Designer: Paul Browning

SUPPLIES
Cardstock (Bazzill Basics); Brown ribbon; Eyelets

"Friendship makes prosperity more shining and lessens adversity by dividing and sharing it." – Cicero

Quick tool

Use a colour wheel if you are not confident about matching colours

SINEAD HOLMES
Designer: Paul Browning

SUPPLIES
Cardstock (Bazzill Basics); Inkpad (VersaColor); Red ribbon; Purple ribbon; Button

Album bites

There is no rule which says your layouts need to be complicated to look good. They can mirror your personal style, which may mean clean, fresh and uncluttered. It is often a reflection of how you decorate your home, or what your favourite shop is! So for Ikea fans everywhere...

Design idea

Use magazines as sources of inspiration for your layouts. Challenge yourself to use one element and incorporate it into your own design

LARKING IN THE LAKES
Designer: Paul Browning

SUPPLIES
Cardstock (Bazzill Basics)

Quick tip

There are many ways to manipulate cardstock – dry embossing, crumpling, burning and painting. Create your own effects without a sheet of patterned paper in sight!

JOHN & PAUL
Designer: Paul Browning

SUPPLIES
Cardstock (Bazzill Basics)

Design shortcut

If you love a quote, why not make a feature of it? They don't have to be tucked away in a corner

KRAZY GANG
Designer: Paul Browning

SUPPLIES
Cardstock (Bazzill Basics)

OUR CLOSE FRIENDS

Designer: Paul Browning

SUPPLIES

Cardstock (Bazzill Basics)

Design shortcut

Use techniques you have mastered in other crafts on your scrapbook layouts – quilting, stitching, folding, altering etc – as these all cross over well onto your pages

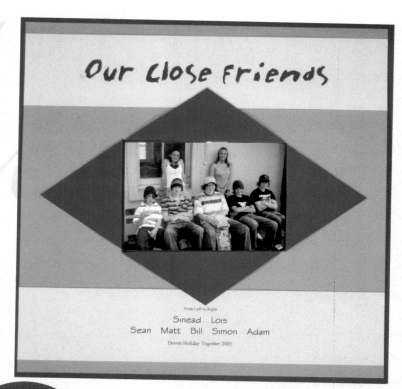

Our Close Friends

From Left to Right
Sinead Lois
Sean Matt Bill Simon Adam
Devon Holiday Together 2005

"You were the one who made things different, you were the one who took me in. You were the one thing I could count on, above all, you were my friend."

- Tom Petty

JOHN

Quick tip

Why not try using the clear backing film from rub-ons in place of acetate, to create windows or clear overlay effects

JOHN

Designer: Paul Browning

SUPPLIES

Cardstock (Bazzill Basics); Inkpad (VersaCraft); Alphabet punches

BEST MATE

AMY NADE

AMY & NADE

Designer: Paul Browning

SUPPLIES

Cardstock (Bazzill Basics); Alphabet stamps (Darice); Mount board; Fibres; Eyelets

Scrapbooking in a weekend REVEALED!

Paul Browning

"When I want to complete an album I always…

Plan my layouts out beforehand, using a computer (I recommend Microsoft Publisher). I've seen others use quick pen and paper sketches which are just as useful. I start out on the screen with a grid (giving nine equal sized squares). A general design rule is to place your main focus of attention on one of these thirds. This is not something I adhere to all the time, but if I'm doing a weekend book it cuts down lots of time in deciding where to place photos etc.

Plan how many pages you want to make beforehand. It may be obvious to say, but choose your photos too. Don't start the weekend by trawling through all your stacks of photos – it can use up a whole day in itself.

Learn to love simplicity. Let your layouts 'breathe'. A single photo and some journaling is all you need.

Use a monochrome colour scheme. This eliminates the time taken to choose papers which go together. I find this is the aspect which can daunt people and consume their time. Three hours choosing papers, one hour making the page (sound familiar? Happens to me too, and I've even studied colour theory).

In the main, use techniques you're familiar with. Don't try to experiment on every page with new ideas you've picked up. If it goes wrong, you will waste time having to do it over again. Save these ideas for pages you can spend more time on later."

MEN BEHAVING MADLY

Designer: Paul Browning

SUPPLIES

Cardstock (Bazzill Basics); Fibres

Design shortcut

Mount the photo with only three sides of tape to leave a pocket for a tag. Set an eyelet and attach fibre to the tag and pop it into the pocket behind the photo

THE BEST OF FRIENDS

Designer: Paul Browning

SUPPLIES

Cardstock (Bazzill Basics); Rubberstamp E2097 Dot Pattern (Hero Arts); Inkpads (VersaColor); Mount board

"If you can dream it, you can do it." - Walt Disney

PUPPIES *Designer: Shalae Tippetts, Scrap Girls*

SUPPLIES USED ON THE WHOLE ALBUM Journaling Biggie (Valerie Randall); Say It brads (Mandy Steward); ScrapSimple Layer Your Own: Stitches Brushes (Mandy Steward); Cafe Sorbet papers (Ann Hetzel Gunkel); ScrapSimple Digital Layout Templates: Stamped! (Ann Hetzel Gunkel); ScrapSimple Paper Templates: Pets Paper Biggie (Ann Hetzel Gunkel); ScrapSimple Digital Layout Templates: Layered Windows 1 (Rozanne Paxman); Atlantis paper (Durin Eberhart); Chocolate Kisses paper (Shalae Tippetts)

Album bites

Digital is on the increase. It is now the way we watch TV, and is certainly the way a lot of us take our photos. Using software packages to create digital elements, print-outs and even entire layouts is now a popular accompaniment and alternative to scrapbooking with paper. Here we take a sneaky peek into a digital album, and see how easy it is to transfer everything you know from paper onto your hard drive

One snowy, November Sunday evening we heard crying in our shed. Imagine our surprise when we found 6 puppies! We managed to find a home for one of them with a neighbor, one of them ran away and these are the four that were left. The kids were in love.

GIDGET *Designer: Shalae Tippetts, Scrap Girls*

Our cockapoo, Gidget, immediately decided that she was the pup's mother and had to be in on everything they did. If they didn't mind her, she would sit on their heads until they got the idea. We kept them in a cardboard box in the basement until they were big enough to be outside. What a mess!

James, Andrew, and Julianne with the puppies.

JAMES & FRIENDS
Designer: Shalae Tippetts, Scrap Girls

We eventually were able to find homes for two more pups, but two of them, Cookie and Spot, became permanent family members. They were particularly loved by James and the pups loved to follow him as he worked.

Design shortcut

Digital scrapbooking is a speedy and inexpensive way of creating layouts and gives you the ability to edit your designs again and again

Quick tip

Don't depend upon your computer hard drive to store photos, supplies and layouts for you. Hard drives fail routinely and you will be very dismayed if you lose all of your precious photos because you didn't have a back-up plan. You should store files on an external hard drive, burn multiple copies of back-up CDs and print layouts out to store in albums

Design shortcut

Many digital scrapbookers enjoy using their digital supplies as printables so that they can make paper layouts, cards and altered projects. Digital supplies print out very nicely on your own printer for use on traditional layouts

Quick tip

While the standard size for creating digital scrapbook layouts is 12x12", many people reduce the file size to 8x8" prior to printing as this will fit on regular-sized photo paper, can be printed out on a regular-sized printer, and fits into readily available 8x8"albums

One of the pups, Spot, seemed to have a sense of humor. He was ready for whatever James wanted to do, even if that meant he would become a puppy Ninja.

It was just part of the fun and Spot was up for fun!

SPOT
Designer: Shalae Tippetts, Scrap Girls

COOKIE & SPOT
Designer:
Rozanne Paxman,
Scrap Girls

....

I was personally the happiest when the pups were asleep. That meant that nothing was being chewed on, nobody was being barked at, the cows weren't being chased, and our yard was safe from new holes.

cookie & spot

PLAYING PUPS
Designer:
Rozanne Paxman,
Scrap Girls

....

Although Cookie & Spot's lives were cut short by someone who didn't value them as we did, this is how our family will always remember them... playing and having fun.

Scrapbooking in a weekend REVEALED!

Ro's top five tips to completing an album in a weekend:

Rozanne Paxman

"1. Gather your pictures together and edit them as necessary.

2. Gather your materials, choosing colours that will work together and complement your photos.

3. Outline the story that you wish to tell with your album and divide the story into reasonable chunks. This will help you determine how many layouts you will need.

4. Create the layouts, using thematic elements such as colours, papers, or embellishments that are used throughout the album to tie it together. Remember to leave the open spots you need for the story.

5. Add the story blocks to the appropriate pages."

Quick tip

You can reuse digital scrapbooking materials that you have purchased, as long as you are using them for your own personal scrapbooking and are not sharing your supplies with your friends, as to do so would break the terms of the licensing agreement. This means that your supplies never run out because they are image files!

Quick Albums

Time-saving tricks and tools for finishing albums now regularly feature on shop shelves. Manufacturers are tailoring new products to the busy scrapbooker and here are just a few of their ideas...

JUST ADD PHOTOS!

The entire-album-in-a-box approach from sei includes everything you need, from the actual album to co-ordinating papers, card, embellishments, stickers and accessories. Just add photos and a little imagination – project done!

GETTING THE MIX RIGHT

On more than one occasion you will find yourself with photos that don't quite fit in your layout designs. The nifty Bay Box system from Scrapworks combines the best of both worlds by organising your loose photos alongside your scrapbooked pages. As well as layouts and photos, the side opening pockets are the perfect hiding place for notes, postcards and little nick-nacks that are as much a part of a memory as the photo.

QUICK KITS

One way to preserve your memories in minutes is by using manufacturers' pre-assembled kits. The kits from Chatterbox, Doodlebug Design and Pebbles Inc come complete with all the components you need to create several layouts. The ideas and layout suggestions on the packaging are also a valuable resource to kick-start your creativity.

WHO SAYS YOU HAVE TO DO ALL THE WORK?

The new idea from Bazzill Basics is to use your friends and relatives to help complete a cover-to-cover album in one fell swoop. By requesting a page or two each from invited participants, you can 'share' the load of scrapbooking and, at the same time, create a very personal montage involving your nearest and dearest.

Remember!

In addition to the helpful products available, look out for the time-saving revelations from our design team. We have plenty of shortcuts, tips, tricks and quick techniques to help you achieve a beautiful finished album in a weekend.

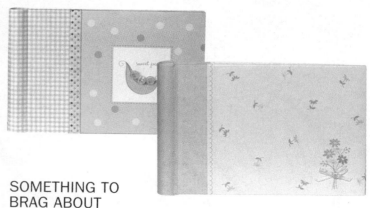

SOMETHING TO BRAG ABOUT

For a quick mini book, there is always the brag option. These handy little keepsakes are perfect to carry around filled with photos of your loved ones and take a fraction of the time to create.

Our Heritage

> "*I have but one lamp by which my feet are guided, and that is the lamp of experience. I know no way of judging of the future but by the past.*" – Edward Gibbon

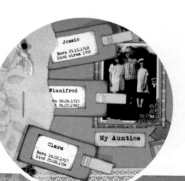

THE WISEMANS
Designer: Kirsty Wiseman

SUPPLIES
Cardstock (Prism); Paper (Hot Off The Press); Pre-strung tags; Hat pin

MY AUNTIES *Designer: Kirsty Wiseman*

SUPPLIES Cardstock (Prism); Paper (Hot Off The Press); Sticker (Pebbles Inc); Flowers (Prima); Lace; Buttons; Hat pin; Staples; Metal corner embellishment

JESSIE *Designer: Kirsty Wiseman*

SUPPLIES Cardstock (Prism); Flowers (Prima); Brads, book label & buckle charm (Making Memories); Computer-printed words and letters; Ribbon

MY MUM, LILLIAN BROWN
Designer: Kirsty Wiseman

SUPPLIES

Cardstock (Prism); Paper (Paper Adventures);
Lace; Brass bonnet charm; Brass button;
Computer-printed title strip; Staples

Quick tips

Staples are useful for attaching twill in
small spaces and also for adding pockets in
which to keep journaling strips

As the space is so small, Kirsty stuck
journaling onto strips to make the page less
crowded and, at the same time, add a
kinetic element

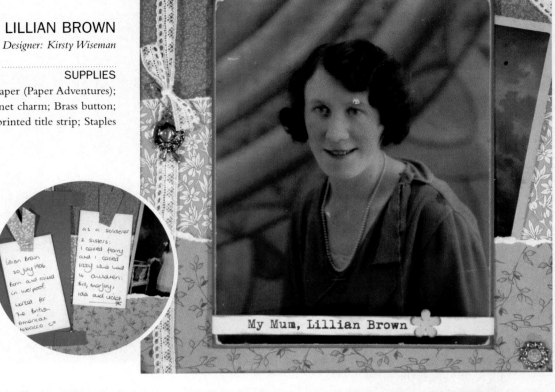

My Mum, Lillian Brown

3 BROTHERS *Designer: Kirsty Wiseman*

SUPPLIES Cardstock (Prism); Paper (BasicGrey); Stickers
(Stickopotamous); Hangerz (Junkitz); Computer-printed journaling;
Alphabet stickers

My Dad, Frederick Wiseman

MY DAD, FREDERICK WISEMAN *Designer: Kirsty Wiseman*

SUPPLIES Cardstock (Prism); Paper (Daisy D's, Hot Off The Press);
Twill (PaperArtsy); Staples; Printed title strips; Watch parts;
Brass clock hands charm

FRED AND LILLIAN
Designer: Kirsty Wiseman

SUPPLIES
Cardstock (Bazzill Basics); Paper (My Mind's Eye);
Flowers (Prima); Brad (Making Memories); Gold trim
(PaperArtsy); Brass button; Computer-printed titles

Photo tip

Using original photos in your layouts can
be a risky business. **Do not** cut them, and
ensure you have copies either saved to disk or
from the developers. Many old photos have details written on the
back of them which, as a part of the history, are well worth
preserving. A clever way to keep the writing is to hinge the photo
onto your page, not sticking it down flat. This way you will still access
the vital notes from your ancestors!

LEONARD
Designer: Kirsty Wiseman

SUPPLIES
Cardstock (Prism); Paper (Hot Off The Press, FoofaLa, Daisy
D's); Twill (PaperArtsy); Buckle (QuicKutz); Photo corners
(Chatterbox); Printed titles & letters; Ribbon; Paperclip

BABY DAVID
Designer: Kirsty Wiseman

SUPPLIES
Cardstock (Prism); Paper (Hot Off The Press);
Rubberstamp Words, plate 5 (PaperArtsy);
Brad (K&Co); Ribbon; Alpha stickers;
Antique bull clip; Heritage rub-ons; Buttons

Designer idea

No die-cut boats? Cut your own simply by shaping
two triangles and a boat base from cardstock. Stick a
star on for decoration

BROTHERS *Designer: Kirsty Wiseman*

SUPPLIES Cardstock (Prism, We R Memory Keepers); Mini Calendar (Hot
Off The Press); Postcard (PaperArtsy); Buckle (Sizzix); Embroidery thread;
Alphabet beads; Purple organza ribbon

FRIENDS *Designer: Kirsty Wiseman*

SUPPLIES Cardstock (Prism); Paper (Daisy D's); Large
punch (Woodware); Black ribbon; Black rickrack;
Alpha letters; Cream tag

BUTLINS
Designer: Kirsty Wiseman

....

SUPPLIES

Cardstock (Prism); Paper (My Mind's Eye, Daisy D's); Hand-cut title (Craft Robo); Fabulous 50s font; Die-cut envelope; Chalk; Photo turns

*Butlins
Skegness*

*Auntie Jessie
Uncle Bill
Mum
Dad
Me*

Lots of Fun!

Quick tip
....

Hand-cut photo corners take seconds to create and can be colour co-ordinated to your layouts by inking or using scraps of the same colour

thinking of days gone by

len married Eileen in Bridlington in 1961

My beloved Brother
Leonard

b. 14 Nov 1936
d. 11 Nov 1988

Len

Quick tool
....

Use a Craft Robo to cut out letters you would not necessarily be able to buy in a commercial alphabet die set

Design shortcut
....

When multi-layering paper, leave un-adhered edges to make invisible pockets in which to store photos and extra memorabilia

LEN
Designer: Kirsty Wiseman

....

SUPPLIES

Cardstock (Prism); Paper (sei); Clock charms; Picot-edged ribbon

Scrapbooking in a weekend REVEALED!

"When I want to save time creating an album I...

* Plan in advance.
* Use a wallet to store photos and discuss the photographs with all the family to obtain as much history as can be recollected.

Kirsty Wiseman

* Write down dates and events in a notebook.
* Plan the album in date order if possible.
* Set aside your 'album weekend'.
* Draw sketches and choose paper that you know will work with your photographs (an 8x8" album is perfect for a heritage album because the photos from the past often seem to be smaller)."

Quick cheat

The ribbon running along the bottom is one long length with a smaller piece made into a knot. This saves having to tie the ribbon onto the paper, risking curling the edges

NO. 85
Designer: Kirsty Wiseman

SUPPLIES

Cardstock (Prism);
Paper (Chatterbox);
Ribbon (May Arts);
Brown acrylic paint;
Star punch;
Circle punch

GARDENER
Designer: Kirsty Wiseman

SUPPLIES
Cardstock (Prism);
Paper (Hot Off The Press); Die-cuts (Hot Off The Press); Ribbon;
Tool charms;
Manilla envelopes

In every conceivable manner, the family is a link to our past and a bridge to our future." - Alex Haley

TABLE OF CONTENTS
Designer: Shauna Berglund-Immel, Hot Off The Press

SUPPLIES
Paper Pizazz patterned paper (HOTP); 8x8" Heritage cardstock (HOTP); Classic Embellish-abilities (HOTP); Slide Mount Mania (HOTP); Family Vinyl Word Block (HOTP); Embroidery thread (DMC); Black Gelly Roll pen (Sakura); Brilliance inkpad (Tsukineko); Foam mounting tape (Scotch); Tattered Lace font (Two Peas in a Bucket); Mini Glue Dots

MOTHER: DEDICATION PAGE
Designer: Shauna Berglund-Immel, Hot Off The Press

SUPPLIES
Paper Pizazz patterned paper (HOTP); 8x8" Heritage cardstock (HOTP); Classic Embellish-abilities (HOTP); Slide Mount Mania (HOTP); Family Vinyl Word Block (HOTP); 12x12" Mother Overlay (HOTP); Embroidery thread (DMC); Black Gelly Roll pen (Sakura); Brilliance inkpad (Tsukineko); Foam mounting tape (Scotch); Tattered Lace font (Two Peas in a Bucket); Mini Glue Dots

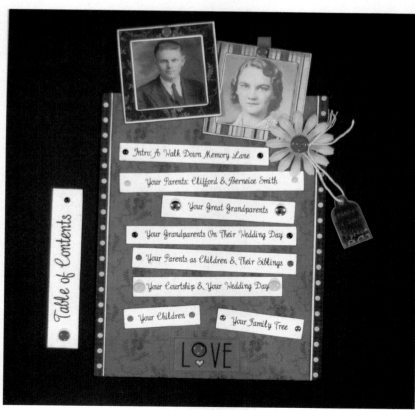

Album bites

A book usually starts with a contents page, and your album can use the same principal to help guide the reader through the pages, as well as give you direction. We recommend:

* Using small strips of journaled text (use a computer or your own handwriting) secured with a variety of brads for added dimension and interest

* Frame clipped photos of the album's subjects in slide mount frames, which will create a visual aspect to the page

* Remember – even though your table of contents is the 2nd page in the album, save it until last in case your design changes

A WALK DOWN MEMORY LANE
Designer: Shauna Berglund-Immel, Hot Off The Press

SUPPLIES
Paper Pizazz patterned paper (HOTP); 8x8" Heritage cardstock (HOTP); Classic Embellish-abilities (HOTP); Slide Mount Mania (HOTP); Family Vinyl Word Block (HOTP); Embroidery thread (DMC); Black Gelly Roll pen (Sakura); Brilliance inkpad (Tsukineko); Tattered Lace font (Two Peas in a Bucket); Mini Glue Dots; Cardstock

Clever journaling

Get personal! Introduce the main characters in your heritage album, giving detailed background information from their own perspectives. Highlight them by adding photos framed with slide mounts. Frame black and white or sepia photos with bright colours like red to help them stand out against a dark background. Repeat the photos on each page, constantly tying them to the story

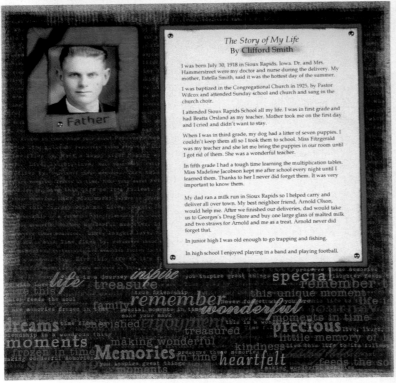

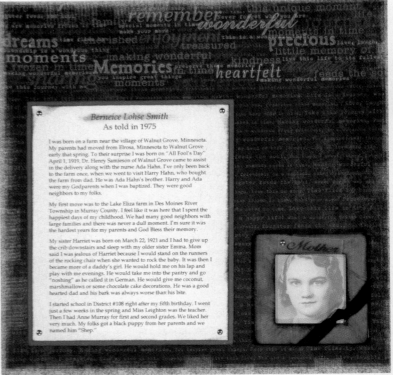

THE STORY OF MY LIFE BY CLIFFORD & BERNEICE LOHSE SMITH *Designer: Shauna Berglund-Immel, Hot Off The Press*

SUPPLIES Paper Pizazz patterned paper (HOTP); 8x8" Heritage & Christmas cardstock (HOTP); Classic Embellish-abilities (HOTP); Slide Mount Mania (HOTP); Family Vinyl Word Block (HOTP); Embroidery thread (DMC); Black Gelly Roll pen (Sakura); Brilliance inkpad (Tsukineko); Tattered Lace font (Two Peas in a Bucket); Foam mounting tape (Scotch); Chalk (Craf-T Products); Mini Glue Dots

My grandparents, John & Hebbe Lohse came to Southbrook Township in 1895. They originally came from Schleswig, Germany. I remember Grandma Lohse sitting in her platform rocker out by the lilac bushes south of the house which were always a ray of beauty in the spring.

— Berneice

Thomas & Harriet Smith and their son, George.

The Smith home was always a place where everyone was welcome. Mrs. Smith fed many a fellow who came to the door for a hand out. There were also many school parties and beautiful weddings at this home that Thomas and his father built.

HOME SWEET HOME *Designer: Shauna Berglund-Immel, Hot Off The Press*

SUPPLIES Paper Pizazz patterned paper (HOTP); 8x8" Heritage & Christmas cardstock (HOTP); Classic Embellish-abilities (HOTP); Slide Mount Mania (HOTP); Family Vinyl Word Block (HOTP); Embroidery thread (DMC); Black Gelly Roll pen (Sakura); Brilliance inkpad (Tsukineko); Foam mounting tape (Scotch); Chalk (Craf-T Products); Mini Glue Dots; Permanent black pen; Staples; Cardstock

My Parents by Clifford Smith

George & Estella met while George was working for a neighbor by the name of Johnny Tapp. Estella had come to visit her grandparents, the Tapp's, and George was invited to a party in her honor. From that day on they became very good friends. After much correspondence, George & Estella were married December 29, 1903 at the home of her parents in Vesta, Minnesota.

George & Estella Smith

Henry & Lena Lohse

My Parents by Berneice Smith

Henry D. Lohse & Lena Anna Koerlin were married March 21, 1912 at the German Lutheran Church in Westbrook, Minnesota, after lent services in the evening. Their attendants were August Lohse, Henry's brother, and Emma Koerlin, Lena's sister.

CLIFF AND BERNEICE'S PARENTS *Designer: Shauna Berglund-Immel, Hot Off The Press*

SUPPLIES Paper Pizazz patterned paper (HOTP); 8x8" Heritage & Christmas cardstock (HOTP); Classic Embellish-abilities (HOTP); Slide Mount Mania (HOTP); Family Vinyl Word Block (HOTP); Embroidery thread (DMC); Brilliance inkpad (Tsukineko); Tattered Lace font (Two Peas in a Bucket); Foam mounting tape (Scotch); Chalk (Craf-T Products); Black Gelly Roll pen (Sakura); Mini Glue Dots

FAMILY PICTURES *Designer: Shauna Berglund-Immel, Hot Off The Press*

SUPPLIES Paper Pizazz patterned paper (HOTP); 8x8" Heritage & Christmas cardstock (HOTP); Classic Embellish-abilities (HOTP); Slide Mount Mania (HOTP); Family Vinyl Word Block (HOTP); Embroidery thread (DMC); Brilliance inkpad (Tsukineko); Tattered Lace font (Two Peas in a Bucket); Foam mounting tape (Scotch); Black Gelly Roll pen (Sakura); 1/16" hole punch (McGill); Mini Glue Dots; Staples; Cardstock

Photo tip

When choosing what colours to matt your photos on, take a look at the background paper you're using and then look at the photo to see whether it is predominately light or dark. Choose a colour that contrasts with the photo, such as a white matt with a dark photo on dark paper. This will prevent your photos from getting lost on the page

LOVE

Designer: Shauna Berglund-Immel, Hot Off The Press

SUPPLIES

Paper Pizazz patterned paper (HOTP); 8x8" Heritage cardstock (HOTP); Classic Embellish-abilities (HOTP); Love Overlay (HOTP); Brilliance inkpad (Tsukineko); Mini Glue Dots; Cardstock

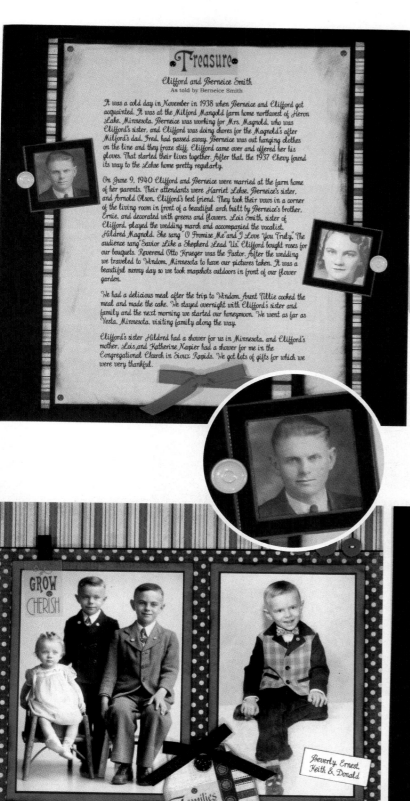

TREASURE

Designer: Shauna Berglund-Immel, Hot Off The Press

SUPPLIES

Paper Pizazz patterned paper (HOTP); 8x8" Heritage & Christmas cardstock (HOTP); Classic Embellish-abilities (HOTP); Slide Mount Mania (HOTP); Family Vinyl Word Block (HOTP); Brilliance inkpad (Tsukineko); Tattered Lace font (Two Peas in a Bucket); Mini Glue Dots; Cardstock

THE SMITH FAMILY

Designer: Shauna Berglund-Immel, Hot Off The Press

SUPPLIES

Paper Pizazz patterned paper (HOTP); 8x8" Heritage & Christmas cardstock (HOTP); Classic Embellish-abilities (HOTP); Slide Mount Mania (HOTP); Family Vinyl Word Block (HOTP); Embroidery thread (DMC); Tattered Lace font (Two Peas in a Bucket); Foam mounting tape (Scotch); 1/16" hole punch (McGill); Mini Glue Dots; Staples; Cardstock

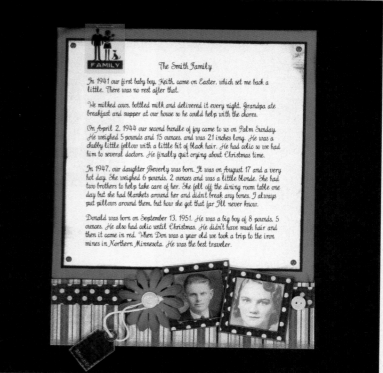

Scrapbooking in a weekend REVEALED!

Shauna Berglund-Immel

"When I want to reach the finishing line I...

- Pre-plan the pages of my album before the weekend, lining out the story I want to tell and the photos I need to tell it. Scan or photocopy, size and print your photos, then put them in a sheet protector for each page of the album – remember that large photos help fill a larger portion of your page, meaning less time to take for embellishing and journaling. Select your papers and co-ordinating embellishments and put them in with the photos.

- Using a book of co-ordinating papers is a simple way to make sure your album maintains a colour scheme and consistency. I chose the Classic Sarapapers collection in the red, black, ecru and ivory color scheme. These papers work well for heritage as they hint at fabrics and textures from the past and are timeless and easy to use.

- Pre-cut and bag food and munchies in snack-sized servings so you can eat and work throughout the weekend. Have plenty of bottled water, caffeine and chocolate on hand to fuel your creativity. Order take-out to be delivered to save on food prep time and clean-up. Once you start scrapping, ignore the phone and answer the door only for your take-out delivery!"

FAMILY TREE

Designer: Shauna Berglund-Immel, Hot Off The Press

SUPPLIES

Paper Pizazz patterned paper (HOTP); 8x8" Heritage & Christmas cardstock (HOTP); Classic Embellish-abilities (HOTP); Slide Mount Mania (HOTP); Family Vinyl Word Block (HOTP); Brilliance inkpad (Tsukineko); Tattered Lace font (Two Peas in a Bucket); Foam mounting tape (Scotch); Mini Glue Dots; Cardstock

"Every man is a quotation from all his ancestors." — Ralph Waldo Emerson

Nellie Taylor
Designer: Katie Shanahan-Jones

SUPPLIES Embossed stickers (K&Co); Studio K transfers (K&Co); 11x8½" paper pad (K&Co); Towering Type (K&Co); Cardstock (Bazzill Basics); Got Flowers? (Prima); Tim Holtz distress ink (Ranger)

HAROLD
Designer: Katie Shanahan-Jones

SUPPLIES Metal Art brads (K&Co); Embossed stickers (K&Co); Studio K transfers (K&Co); 11x8½" paper pad (K&Co); Cardstock (Bazzill Basics); Eliza font (QuicKutz); Tim Holtz stamps (Stampers Anonymous); Tim Holtz distress ink & embossing powder (Ranger)

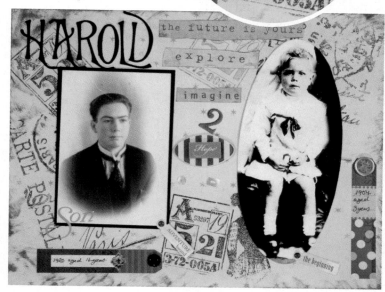

A LIFE IN SERVICE
*Designer:
Katie Shanahan-Jones*

SUPPLIES 11x8½" paper pad (K&Co); Cardstock (Bazzill Basics)

Album bites

Scrapbooking in the 21st century began in earnest after a conference on Family History (aka Genealogy). Seeking out our ancestors has become one of the motivating factors in the growth of the hobby, as well as the topic for TV shows, internet sites and magazines. It seems that we can't get enough of digging out our past and recording it

KATE – DEVOTED WIFE
Designer: Katie Shanahan-Jones

SUPPLIES Studio K transfers (K&Co); 11x8½" paper pad (K&Co); Towering Type (K&Co); Cardstock (Bazzill Basics); Got Flowers? (Prima); Katie font (QuicKutz); Tim Holtz distress ink (Ranger); Twill (7gypsies)

Quick tip

Use softer, lighter colours to give your pages a more feminine feel

Quick tool

Use die-cutting machines to make quick titles for your pages

LOVE
Designer: Katie Shanahan-Jones

SUPPLIES Embossed stickers (K&Co); 12x12" flat papers (K&Co); Studio K Transfers (K&Co); 11x8½" paper pad (K&Co); Cardstock (Bazzill Basics); Photo corners (QuicKutz); Tim Holtz distress ink (Ranger)

Quick tools

Use Hermafix or another dry adhesive such as double-sided tape. It may seem obvious, but it saves so much time and effort because you are not waiting for glue to dry before moving onto the next page

GOING HOME
Designer: Katie Shanahan-Jones

SUPPLIES Metal Art brads (K&Co); Embossed stickers (K&Co); 12x12" flat papers (K&Co); 11x8½" paper pad (K&Co); Tim Holtz distress ink (Ranger); Photo corners

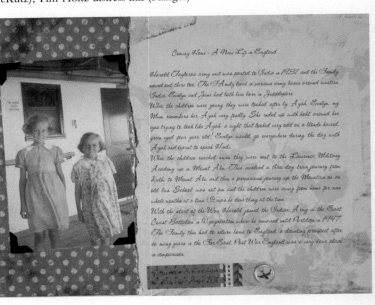

EXPERIENCE HAPPINESS
Designer: Katie Shanahan-Jones

SUPPLIES 12x12" flat papers (K&Co); 11x8½" paper pad (K&Co); Tim Holtz distress ink (Ranger); Cardstock tags (Making Memories); mini brads (Making Memories); Cardstock (Bazzill Basics)

Design shortcut

If you use smaller pages (rather than 12x12) you will be able to print directly onto the pages, as a smaller size will fit most printers!

LITTLE DAVID
Designer: Katie Shanahan-Jones

SUPPLIES Metal Art brads (K&Co); 11x8½" paper pad (K&Co); Tim Holtz distress ink (Ranger); Cardstock (Bazzill Basics)

Quick tip

Use muted colours and minimal embellishments to portray a strong masculine and simple look

Clever journaling

If you are nervous about writing directly onto a layout then DON'T! Instead, create a journaling block and write on there. It's dispensable if you do make a mistake, and you don't stick it down until you are 100% happy with it

TO DAD
Designer: Katie Shanahan-Jones

SUPPLIES 11x8½" paper pad (K&Co); Tim Holtz distress ink (Ranger); Cardstock (Bazzill Basics); Staples

A CHANGE OF CAREER
Designer: Katie Shanahan-Jones

SUPPLIES Embossed stickers (K&Co); 11x8½" paper pad (K&Co); Towering Type (K&Co); Cardstock (Bazzill Basics); Got Flowers? (Prima); Tim Holtz distress ink (Ranger)

Design idea

Heritage doesn't need to be dull! Sometimes it's all too easy to clump Family History and Heritage into the beige and brown category, and miss some of the colourful details that are our past! Adding softer, lighter colours adds a more feminine feel, and this can be enhanced by also including floral and girly embellishments to create a prettier look

LOVE (1953)
Designer: Katie Shanahan-Jones

SUPPLIES Metal Art brads (K&Co); Embossed stickers (K&Co); 12x12" flat papers (K&Co); Studio K transfers (K&Co); Tim Holtz distress ink (Ranger); Cardstock (Bazzill Basics); Ribbon (May Arts); Got Flowers? (Prima)

Quick tip

Emphasise important words Use several sizes of stickers in various styles to place emphasis on words showing expression, action or special importance to the layout

Quick tip

Create dimension. Change your letter heights by adhering a few of the letters from a word on pop-dots or buttons. You could also put a clear page pebble over the top of a letter sticker

ENFORCED ABSENCES
Designer: Katie Shanahan-Jones

SUPPLIES Embossed stickers (K&Co); Studio K transfers (K&Co); 11x8½" paper pad (K&Co); Cardstock (Bazzill Basics); Tim Holtz Epoxy Stickerz (Junkitz)

GERMANY (1958)
Designer: Katie Shanahan-Jones

SUPPLIES Embossed stickers (K&Co); Studio K transfers (K&Co); 11x8½" paper pad (K&Co); Emily & Ginger fonts (QuicKutz); Cardstock (Bazzill Basics); Cardstock tags (Making Memories); Mini brads (Making Memories); Tim Holtz distress ink (Ranger)

SINGAPORE
Designer: Katie Shanahan-Jones

SUPPLIES Metal Art brads (K&Co); Embossed stickers (K&Co); Studio K transfers (K&Co); 11x8½" paper pad (K&Co); Lucy font (QuicKutz); Cardstock (Bazzill Basics); Tim Holtz distress ink (Ranger); Parasol; Photo corners

Scrapbooking in a weekend REVEALED!

Katie's tips for completing an album in a weekend:

★ Have a plan for your scrapbook before you start. For example, I chose to tell a story, which made choosing the photos and completing the journaling much more straightforward!

★ Spend time before you start scrapping choosing and printing out your photographs. The right photos should inspire each layout.

★ Try creating an album in chronological order – it will make the flow of the layouts more natural.

★ Buy a set of themed or collection papers from one manufacturer so you don't waste time looking for matching papers.

★ If you buy two or three packs of embellishments that co-ordinate with your papers it saves time, and by keeping the embellishments simple the end result looks more stylish.

★ Scrap in a size smaller than the usual 12x12 to make your scrapbook quicker to produce.

★ Don't sweat about the little stuff – think of the end result you want to achieve and this will keep you focused."

Katie Shanahan-Jones

Getting organised

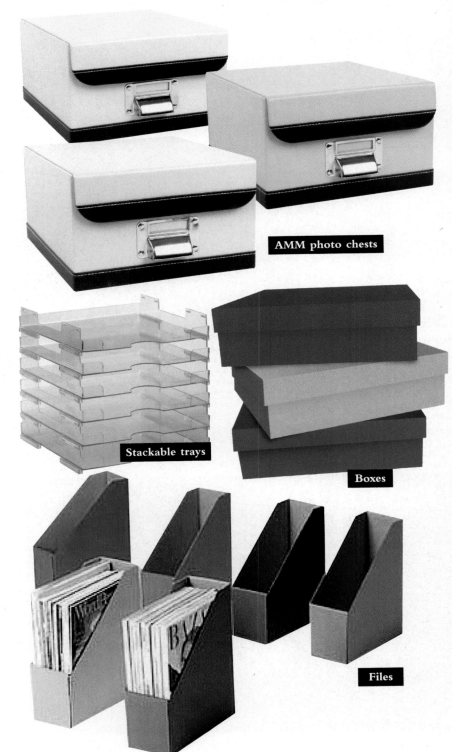

AMM photo chests

Stackable trays

Boxes

Files

As a scrapbooker, one of the biggest drains on your time is not knowing where specific supplies are located. Being organised can be a challenge to begin with, but your creativity will benefit as a result and you will become more effective in reaching those important 'finishing lines' with your layouts and albums

THE ACTION PLAN

1. Sort

Grouping supplies into categories is the best starting point. Put all your paper, adhesives, pens, tools, templates, rub-ons, stickers etc in their own boxes, containers and files. Organise them by theme if you have the dedication!

2. Label

Once items are grouped, label them clearly.

3. Define space

Define your work space and have everything located close by. Not all of us can have craft rooms or even tables allocated specifically for our hobby, but all you need is a small cupboard or corner to make a difference.

4. Throw away

It may be painful, but throw away (or donate) any supplies you won't use or no longer like. Use online auction sites if they are high value, or donate to kids' clubs or schools. A good purge will clear out the clutter and give you a clear idea of what you have to work with.

5. Storage

Time to shop… as if you needed an excuse! Buy tins, stackable containers, filing and shelving to provide the right kind of long-term storage to keep supplies both safe and organised. The storage solutions don't need to be scrapbook specific – try looking in DIY or home office shops for cheap clear boxes, or baskets that stack.

6. Stay ahead

Once you have spent the time organising, keep ahead by always putting supplies away in their place. It's a simple thing, and one we drum into the kids, but it makes all the difference when it comes to locating that piece of paper. Don't let your hard work go to waste!

Seasons

"Christmas! Tis the season for kindling the fire of hospitality in the hall, the genial fire of charity in the heart." – Washington Irving

All hearts come home for Christmas,
across the miles and years.
To live again the age old joys
that passing time endears.
All hearts come home for Christmas,
the near and the far...
For home is where the love is found
and where the memories are.

ALL HEARTS COME HOME FOR CHRISTMAS

Designer: Brenda Cosgrove, Pebbles Inc

SUPPLIES

Ribbon (Pebbles Inc); Metal word charm (Pebbles Inc); Patterned paper (Pebbles Inc); CK Higgins Handprint font (2Peas); Cardstock (Bazzill Basics); Chalk inkpad (ColorBox); Staples; Thread

Christmas tree

The Story of our Christmas Tree

We had decided Christmas 2002 not to get a tree because we were going to Canada for Christmas and hate to have the tree up for such a short time before we have to take it down. However, things changed when we were on our way home from church and saw an artificial tree sitting in the front of Peay's yard with a for sale sign on it. Of course Carley and Caitlyn ran right over to check it out and they came home and begged us to get it. We never thought we would ever have an artificial tree, but because the girls were so excited about it we went over to see it. We were very surprised at how beautiful it was. We decided to see what Peays wanted for the tree. When Mom called she was thrilled when Sister Peay told her she could have it for $20. Of course Dad went right over and paid for it and brought it home. We feel like we have been blessed with being able to get such a beautiful tree!

Christmas 2002

CHRISTMAS TREE *Designer: Brenda Cosgrove, Pebbles Inc*

SUPPLIES Ribbon (Pebbles Inc); Metal word charm (Pebbles Inc); Patterned paper (Pebbles Inc); Typo font (2Peas); Cardstock (Bazzill Basics); Chalk inkpad (ColorBox); Staples; Thread

COOKIE EXCHANGE

Designer: Brenda Cosgrove, Pebbles Inc

SUPPLIES

Ribbon (Pebbles Inc); Metal word charm (Pebbles Inc); Patterned paper (Pebbles Inc); CK Higgins Handprint font (2Peas); Cardstock (Bazzill Basics); Chalk inkpad (ColorBox); Staples; Thread

Design shortcut

Before you start adding photos and journaling, prepare each page – here Brenda pre-stitched one edge of her page with zigzag stitches, and inked and sanded her patterned paper

Quick tips

Once ribbon is tied around your page, staple on the edges to secure

Ink around photo matts, and around title and journal blocks

Quick journaling

Scrapbooking is more than photos – it is your chance to leave a footprint on the future by recording simple things about your present. Favourite recipes are one of many everyday 'life notes' that you may take for granted, but your children will cherish

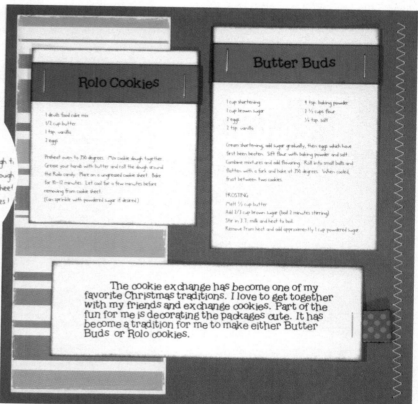

RECIPES

Designer: Brenda Cosgrove, Pebbles Inc

SUPPLIES

Ribbon (Pebbles Inc); Patterned paper (Pebbles Inc); Typo & CK Higgins Handprint fonts (2Peas); Cardstock (Bazzill Basics); Chalk inkpad (ColorBox); Staples; Thread

Decorating the livingroom and the Christmas tree on Thanksgiving Day has become a tradition. Mom loves to get her Christmas room set up. Once it is done we are ready to get in the Christmas spirit. We think our livingroom becomes a magical room at Christmastime.

DECORATIONS

Designer: Brenda Cosgrove, Pebbles Inc

SUPPLIES

Ribbon (Pebbles Inc); Metal word charm (Pebbles Inc); Patterned paper (Pebbles Inc); Typo font (2Peas); Cardstock (Bazzill Basics); Chalk inkpad (ColorBox); Staples; Thread

Quick tip

For this type of album use no more than two or three fonts on a layout. Your lettering is an element of your scrapbook page, but it shouldn't dominate the design

When the kids were little we played Christmas Bingo Christmas Eve. As our kids have got older we have changed the tradition a little, instead of playing Bingo we open a Christmas Eve. (this gift is always a new game for the Christmas Eve. have lots of fun playing the NEW game together.

Christmas is a great time to make treats. A new family favorite is Gourmet Candy Apples. Mom and the girls have decided making these delicious apples is a new tradition!

GAMES/SWEETS

Designer: Brenda Cosgrove, Pebbles Inc

SUPPLIES

Ribbon (Pebbles Inc); Patterned paper (Pebbles Inc); Typo font (2Peas); Cardstock (Bazzill Basics); Chalk inkpad (ColorBox); Staples; Thread

MUSIC/CHOCOLATES *Designer: Brenda Cosgrove, Pebbles Inc*

SUPPLIES

Ribbon (Pebbles Inc); Metal word charm (Pebbles Inc); Patterned paper (Pebbles Inc); Typo & CK Higgins Handprint fonts (2Peas); Cardstock (Bazzill Basics); Chalk inkpad (ColorBox); Staples; Thread

Quick tool

Use a CD as part of your layout to include additional photos, or even music downloads of your favourite songs

PAJAMAS
Designer: Brenda Cosgrove, Pebbles Inc

SUPPLIES

Ribbon (Pebbles Inc); Metal word charm (Pebbles Inc); Patterned paper (Pebbles Inc); Typo font (2Peas); Cardstock (Bazzill Basics); Chalk inkpad (ColorBox); Staples; Thread

SNACK FOR SANTA

Designer: Brenda Cosgrove, Pebbles Inc

SUPPLIES

Ribbon (Pebbles Inc); Patterned paper (Pebbles Inc);
Typo font (2Peas); Cardstock (Bazzill Basics); Chalk
inkpad (ColorBox); Staples; Thread

After the socks are hung
the kids get a snack ready to
leave for Santa along with a note.

Christmas 2005

CHRISTMAS EVE DINNER

Designer: Brenda Cosgrove, Pebbles Inc

SUPPLIES

Ribbon (Pebbles Inc); Patterned paper (Pebbles Inc);
Typo font (2Peas); Cardstock (Bazzill Basics);
Chalk inkpad (ColorBox); Staples; Thread

Favorite
Christmas Eve
FOOD

Over the years our Christmas Eve Dinner
has become a tradition and feast everyone
looks forward to. We all enjoy our favorite
finger foods sitting by the cozy fire.

Reading the Christmas Story is something we do every Christmas Eve. When our kids were little we would dress them up in costumes, and have them act out the nativity. Caitlyn even had the chance to be our baby Jesus the year she was born. (having a 5 day old baby at Christmas was wonderful!) As the children have grown, we have begun to watch the Nativity on DVD. It is a favorite time on Christmas Eve for Mom. Being able to sit down as a family and watch the Christmas story helps us to have the spirit of Christmas and remember the birth of Jesus.

Nana made each of us gift boxes. We keep these boxes in greenery by our fireplace. On Christmas Eve after watching the Nativity we each open our box and get the paper out from the year before. On the paper we wrote our "gift" to Christ. (they are usually things we would like to improve in ourselves) After reading what we wrote the year before, we write new "gifts" to Christ.

NATIVITY/GIFTS
Designer: Brenda Cosgrove, Pebbles Inc

SUPPLIES

Ribbon (Pebbles Inc); Metal word charm (Pebbles Inc); Patterned paper (Pebbles Inc); Typo font (2Peas); Cardstock (Bazzill Basics); Chalk inkpad (ColorBox); Staples; Thread

Scrapbooking in a weekend REVEALED!

"My tips for completing an album in a weekend are:

1. Decide on your theme and select the photos. It is really helpful when trying to complete an album in a weekend to choose a theme for the album and then find the photos you want to use. This will save you time as you go along.

2. Select your materials. It is especially helpful for a weekend album to select a co-ordinating line of patterned papers and embellishments.

3. Follow a basic design. Although I knew each of my pages would feature a different tradition, I wanted the pages to co-ordinate. I also wanted a basic design for each, to help me complete the album in a short amount of time.

4. Add simple touches. Little things like stitching, staples, inking and adding ribbon add variety and texture to your album. It will save you time if you do the stitching on your background pages all at once. Also, cutting border strips all together helps reduce time.

5. Use minimal fonts. Sticking to the same few fonts throughout the album not only saves a lot of time, it also helps to tie your album together.

6. Sketch your ideas first. I find that having a plan down on paper helps me when I begin doing my actual pages. I like to sketch my basic design for the album, including the size of the album and the design scheme. Following a basic format and differentiating pages with small touches helps them come together easily."

Brenda Cosgrove

"*I wish we could put up some of t*

Album bites

With all the preparations and stresses of Christmas, it is sometimes easy to lose sight of spending time with family. No matter how prepared you are, there always seems to be a mountain of nagging tasks to be done. So why not treat yourself to a guilt-free family day, taking pictures along the way? It is the perfect opportunity to refocus on what matters most, and get everyone on board for the main event. Create an album around family adventures and the countdown to Christmas and start a new tradition while you're at it!

FRIENDS, JOY, PEACE
Designer: Nicola Clarke

SUPPLIES
Ribbon (Li'l Davis Designs); Patterned paper (Li'l Davis Designs); Painted binder clips (Li'l Davis Designs); Flower (Li'l Davis Designs); Foam stamps (Li'l Davis Designs); Brads (Junkitz); Cardstock (Bazzill Basics); Paint; Staples

CHRISTMAS CARD *Designer: Nicola Clarke*

SUPPLIES Ribbon (Li'l Davis Designs); Patterned paper (Li'l Davis Designs); Bottle caps (Li'l Davis Designs); Silver buckle (Li'l Davis Designs); Patterned & Outline chipboard alphabets (Li'l Davis Designs); Vintage shapes (Li'l Davis Designs); Cardstock (Bazzill Basics); Staples; Sewing thread; Dymo tape

Christmas spirit in jars and open a jar of it every month." – Harlan Miller

Quick tip

Always remember
to add journaling to your pages; it will
help retell memories more completely

Design shortcut

Use page tabs as hinges to lift photographs
and hide journaling

CELEBRATE
Designer: Nicola Clarke

SUPPLIES

Patterned paper (Li'l Davis Designs); Vintage words (Li'l Davis
Designs); Cardstock (Bazzill Basics); Sewing thread; Dymo tape

Quick cheat

To make your paper go further, use a craft knife to cut the
portions of the background paper out which will be
covered by large photos and journaling matts. These can
be used to cover slide mounts and to matt photos onto

NOEL
Designer: Nicola Clarke

SUPPLIES

Patterned paper (Li'l Davis Designs); Vintage shapes (Li'l Davis
Designs); Bottle cap (Li'l Davis Designs); Ribbon (Li'l Davis Designs);
Cardstock (Bazzill Basics); Sewing; Staples; Ink; Dymo tape

FOR SANTA *Designer: Nicola Clarke*

SUPPLIES Patterned paper (Li'l Davis Designs); Vintage shapes (Li'l Davis Designs); Patterned chipboard alphabet (Li'l Davis Designs); Painted binder clip (Li'l Davis Designs); Ribbon (Li'l Davis Designs); Cardstock (Bazzill Basics); Brads (Junkitz); Sewing thread; Staples; Dymo tape

CHRISTMAS EVE *Designer: Nicola Clarke*

SUPPLIES Patterned paper (Li'l Davis Designs); Ribbon (Li'l Davis Designs); Flowers (Li'l Davis Designs); Patterned chipboard alphabet (Li'l Davis Designs); Bottle cap (Li'l Davis Designs); Cardstock (Bazzill Basics); Brads (Junkitz); Sewing thread; Stapler; Dymo tape

OUR WHITE CHRISTMAS
Designer: Nicola Clarke

SUPPLIES
Patterned paper (Li'l Davis Designs); Ribbon (Li'l Davis Designs); Patterned chipboard alphabet (Li'l Davis Designs); Foam stamps (Li'l Davis Designs); Cardstock (Bazzill Basics); Brads (Junkitz); Sewing thread; Paint

Quick technique

Use 3D foam pads to make the titles stand out from the layout

Design idea

Shadow Letters Lightly adhere an alphabet sticker to your page, then paint, ink or chalk over it. When you remove the sticker, you'll have a clean outline of the letter left behind on the paper

DEC 25 *Designer: Nicola Clarke*

SUPPLIES Patterned paper (Li'l Davis Designs); Foam stamps (Li'l Davis Designs); Vintage shapes (Li'l Davis Designs); Flower (Li'l Davis Designs); Cardstock (Bazzill Basics); Sewing thread; Paint; Dymo tape

Quick tip

Try incorporating mini books or cards within your layout or album. At Christmas you often receive annual newsletters and notes from friends and family, and it is worth saving and using them in your Christmas album

BOXING DAY
Designer: Nicola Clarke

SUPPLIES
Patterned paper (Li'l Davis Designs); Foam stamps (Li'l Davis Designs); Outline & Patterned chipboard alphabets (Li'l Davis Designs); Cardstock (Bazzill Basics); Sewing thread; Paint

BEFORE, DURING & AFTER *Designer: Nicola Clarke*

SUPPLIES Patterned paper (Li'l Davis Designs); Foam stamps (Li'l Davis Designs); Bottle caps (Li'l Davis Designs); Patterned chipboard alphabet (Li'l Davis Designs); Painted binder clip (Li'l Davis Designs); Cardstock (Bazzill Basics); Sewing thread; Paint; Dymo tape

MEMORIES OF CHRISTMAS

Designer: Nicola Clarke

SUPPLIES

Patterned paper (Li'l Davis Designs); Foam stamps (Li'l Davis Designs); Bottle cap (Li'l Davis Designs); Patterned & Outline chipboard alphabets (Li'l Davis Designs); Patterned tape (Li'l Davis Designs); Vintage shape (Li'l Davis Designs); Cardstock (Bazzill Basics); Sewing thread; Paint; Staples; Dymo tape

Quick tip

Keeping all your gift receipts isn't just for the January returns! Slipping them into a pocket in your Christmas album will help you remember what was bought and given that year. It's also interesting to see how the prices and value of products change over the years

Ever since I can remember we have been taking family vacations. As a child there was always an annual road trip to Fort Meyers Beach, Florida. This was a 24 hour car adventure with my parents and brother with an overnight stay at South of the Border, followed by a week at Disney, the beach, and then the same 24 hour trip home. As an adult we have continued the tradition with many journeys around the country together. From coast to coast we have seen it all, and the best part was we doing it together. Sharing the experience with family brings us all closer together and gives us great stories to remember for years to come. It was 1997 when we took a trip to Washington DC. From our hotel it was well over 3 miles to the Lincoln Memorial, it seems like we walked for hours to get there and back and our feet hurt for the next two days. We all still talk about this walk like it happened just yesterday. There are countless other stories that we all have in our memories. Sightseeing and traveling is something that always makes me happy, especially when I am with family, and I am hopeful that we will have many more trips to share in the future.

adventure   getaway   sightseeing   vacation

"Once you have travelled, the voyage never ends, but is played out over and over again in the quietest chambers, that the mind can never break off from the journey." - Pat Conroy

FAMILY VACATION
Designer: Missy Neal

SUPPLIES
Patterned paper (Hot Off The Press); Embellish-abilities (Hot Off The Press); Cardmaker's ribbon & accents (Hot Off The Press); Attachments vinyl tags (Hot Off The Press); Fabric stickers (Hot Off The Press)

Album bites

The summer holidays are the perfect time to kick back and relax, whether on an exotic beach or in your own back garden. A whole year can be spent planning the details of your week in the sun, and a camera should be first in the suitcase

YOSEMITE
Designer: Missy Neal

SUPPLIES
Patterned paper (Hot Off The Press); Embellish-abilities (Hot Off The Press); Cardmaker's ribbon & accents (Hot Off The Press); Attachments vinyl tags (Hot Off The Press); Fabric stickers (Hot Off The Press); Definitions & Word Ephemera (Hot Off The Press); Cardstock (Prism); Thread

Quick tip

To make sure the journaling tags don't slide too far behind the photos, add some adhesive to the middle of the photo matt before sticking to the page

LAKE TAHOE
Designer: Missy Neal

SUPPLIES
Patterned paper (Hot Off The Press); Cardmaker's ribbon & accents (Hot Off The Press); Attachments vinyl tags (Hot Off The Press); Fabric stickers (Hot Off The Press); Definitions & Word Ephemera (Hot Off The Press); Cardstock (Prism); Die-cut letters (Sizzix); Floss (DMC)

SAN FRANCISCO *Designer: Missy Neal*

SUPPLIES Patterned paper (Hot Off The Press); Cardmaker's ribbon & accents (Hot Off The Press); Attachments vinyl tags (Hot Off The Press); Fabric stickers (Hot Off The Press); Definitions & Word Ephemera (Hot Off The Press); Cardstock (Prism); Die-cut letters (Sizzix)

Design idea

Customised chipboard letters Cover the top surface of your chipboard letter with glue. Add the patterned paper face up onto the chipboard letters. Roll with a brayer to get a smooth, even coverage of adhesive. Give the glue a few minutes to dry and then cut out each letter using a craft knife. To get the edges nice and clean, rub the edges very lightly with a piece of fine sandpaper. Finally, edge the sides of the letters with ink

SANTA CRUZ
Designer: Missy Neal

SUPPLIES

Patterned paper (Hot Off The Press); Cardmaker's accents (Hot Off The Press); Attachments ribbon set (Hot Off The Press); Tags (Hot Off The Press); Definitions & Word Ephemera (Hot Off The Press); Cardstock (Prism); Chipboard letters

Quick cheat

To quickly thread ribbon through a small hole, use a piece of thin wire bent into a U shape. Place the ribbon between the wire and push it through the hole

NAPA
Designer: Missy Neal

SUPPLIES

Patterned paper (Hot Off The Press); Tags (Hot Off The Press); Embellish-abilities (Hot Off The Press); Cardmaker's ribbon & accents (Hot Off The Press); Slide mounts (Hot Off The Press); Journey Ephemera (Hot Off The Press); Definitions & Word Ephemera (Hot Off The Press); Chipboard letters

Design idea

To get this edge effect, adhere a piece of patterned paper to the background cardstock, keeping the adhesive away from the edges. Then make little tears, ¼–½" long, around the edges and bend back to expose the reverse of the patterned paper. Sew a straight line of stitches around the perimeter, about ¼" in from the edge. Finally, sponge ink over the edge of the paper

CAPE COD

Designer: Missy Neal

SUPPLIES

Patterned paper (Hot Off The Press); Tags (Hot Off The Press); Fabric stickers (Hot Off The Press); Embellish-abilities (Hot Off The Press); Cardmaker's accents (Hot Off The Press); Slide mount (Hot Off The Press); Definitions & Word Ephemera (Hot Off The Press); Cardstock (Prism); Die-cut letters (Sizzix); Thread

Quick tips

If you have a lot of journaling, try adding some to the back of the layout

For a more dramatic look when layering paper, try matting a few layers or all layers with patterned paper

BALTIMORE

Designer: Missy Neal

SUPPLIES

Patterned paper (Hot Off The Press); Tags (Hot Off The Press); Embellish-abilities (Hot Off The Press); Cardmaker's ribbon (Hot Off The Press); Cardstock (Prism); Die-cut letters (Sizzix); Thread

TEXAS *Designer: Missy Neal*

SUPPLIES Patterned paper (Hot Off The Press); Fabric stickers (Hot Off The Press); Embellish-abilities (Hot Off The Press); Cardmaker's ribbon (Hot Off The Press); Slide mounts (Hot Off The Press); Definitions & Word Ephemera (Hot Off The Press); Chipboard letters

Photo tip

If your subject is wearing a bright purple shirt (just for example!) that doesn't match with anything, a quick solution is to convert your picture to black and white

MYSTIC SEAPORT
Designer: Missy Neal

SUPPLIES

Patterned paper (Hot Off The Press); Attachments vinyl tags (Hot Off The Press); Fabric stickers (Hot Off The Press); Cardmaker's accents (Hot Off The Press); Slide mount (Hot Off The Press); Cardstock stickers (Hot Off The Press); Journey Ephemera (Hot Off The Press); Cardstock (Prism); Die-cut alphabet (Sizzix)

easons

POINT REYES
Designer: Missy Neal

....

SUPPLIES
Patterned paper (Hot Off The Press); Attachments ribbon set (Hot Off The Press);
Fabric stickers (Hot Off The Press); Cardmaker's accents (Hot Off The Press);
Slide mounts (Hot Off The Press); Vintage Ephemera (Hot Off The Press);
Cardstock (Prism); Metal-rimmed tag

Quick tip

....

Use hidden tags so that unruly handwriting isn't visible

"My tips for completing an album in a weekend include:

Missy Neal

1. Pre-plan the pictures you want to scrap. It's important to remember that you don't need to scrap every photo that you take – pick your favourites, the ones that make you remember your event, and the ones that help tell your story.

2. Don't be afraid to cut freehand matts around odd-shaped elements. You can save a lot of time if you don't worry about making perfect measurements.

3. If you plan to use stitching on your pages, consider using a neutral colour of thread (white, cream, brown, or black) on all the pages. This will create a uniform look in your album and save you the time of changing the thread on your sewing machine.

4. Rather than spending a lot of time trying to find patterned paper that matches your pictures perfectly, convert your pictures to black and white.

5. You can save time by adding journaling to the back of your layouts – not every page needs to have visible journaling on the front, especially if you don't like the look of your handwritten journaling and don't want to spend time journaling on the computer.

6. Consider making a sketch of your page idea: either make a sketch and then choose the photos to fit, or start with the number and size of photos you want to use and create a sketch with those in mind.

7. Don't worry about filling every inch of space on your layout with an embellishment. Let some of that beautiful patterned paper or cardstock show through."

"Another fresh new year is here…
Another year to live!
To banish worry, doubt, and fear,
To love and laugh and give!"

– William Arthur Ward

Album bites

Creating an album all in one go is much easier if you keep your eye on the 'big picture'. Gathering a couple of photos per month and keeping the page themed to a season makes the finishing line that bit closer!

JANUARY
Designer: Alison Docherty

SUPPLIES
Patterned paper (Karen Foster Design); Cardstock (Prism); Ribbon (Making Memories); Die-cut letters; Thread

FEBRUARY
Designer: Alison Docherty

SUPPLIES
Patterned paper (Karen Foster Design); Cardstock (Prism); Ribbon (May Arts); Paperclips; Die-cut letters; Thread

MARCH

Designer: Alison Docherty

....

SUPPLIES

Patterned paper (Karen Foster Design);
Cardstock (Prism); Die-cut letters;
Brads; Thread

APRIL

Designer: Alison Docherty

....

SUPPLIES

Patterned paper (Karen Foster Design); Cardstock (Prism);
Brads; Die-cut letters; Thread

Design shortcut

....

Break the album down into sections, including backgrounds, photo
matts and journaling. Complete each of the sections across all of the
pages (i.e. design and construct all of the backgrounds first, then matt
all of your photographs and adhere to each page, then complete the
journaling and finally add any embellishments)

Design shortcut

Alison used a sewing machine on her layouts, but you can cheat with sewing-effect rub-ons or even with a pen

Quick tips

Colour co-ordinate your card and paper to the colours in your photos

Recycle sayings and quotes from the inside of old greetings cards

MAY

Designer: Alison Docherty

SUPPLIES

Patterned paper (Karen Foster Design);
Cardstock (Prism); Ribbon (May Arts);
Paperclips; Die-cut letters; Thread

JUNE

Designer: Alison Docherty

SUPPLIES

Patterned paper (Karen Foster Design); Cardstock
(Prism); Ribbon (Making Memories); Paperclips;
Die-cut letters; Thread

JULY

Designer: Alison Docherty

SUPPLIES

Patterned paper (Karen Foster Design);
Cardstock (Prism); Brads; Die-cut letters; Thread

Quick tip

Why not try journaling in a colour
other than black? If you are using your
computer, simply select a change in
the text colour and print on either
patterned or dark paper

Design idea

Try using patterned paper where you would usually opt for plain
cardstock. The effect will be a busier, more colourful layout

Photo tip

At special events make a mental (or written) note beforehand of
the photos you want to take

AUGUST

Designer: Alison Docherty

SUPPLIES

Patterned paper (Karen Foster Design);
Cardstock (Prism); Brads; Die-cut letters; Thread

SEPTEMBER
Designer: Alison Docherty

SUPPLIES
Patterned paper (Karen Foster Design); Cardstock (Prism); Die-cut letters; Brads; Thread

Quick tool

A Xyron machine helps when adhering die-cut letters to your layout, especially as you don't need to wait for any glue to dry

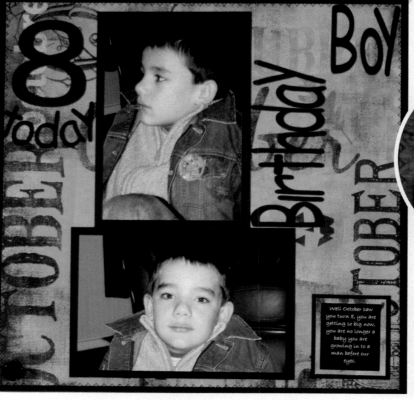

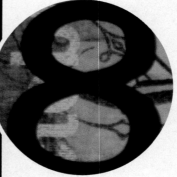

Design shortcut

Keep an album cohesive by using photo matts and embellishments consistently throughout

OCTOBER
Designer: Alison Docherty

SUPPLIES
Patterned paper (Karen Foster Design); Cardstock (Prism); Brads; Die-cut letters; Thread

NOVEMBER
Designer: Alison Docherty

SUPPLIES
Patterned paper (Karen Foster Design); Cardstock (Prism); Ribbon (May Arts); Paperclips; Die-cut letters; Thread

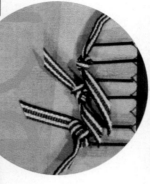

Scrapbooking in a weekend REVEALED!

Alison Docherty

"My tips on how to create an album quickly:

1. Have all your photographs to hand before you start. Either get them printed at a photo shop or print them yourself at home.

2. Print all the photographs in one colourway so that you don't waste time printing some black and white and some in colour. That way you can set your printer off while you start on your layouts.

3. Collect all your supplies together, making sure that you have enough supplies to complete the whole album.

4. Keep the overall design clean and simple so that it easy to reproduce on each page.

5. Plan what pictures will be on each page so you don't spend time leafing through photographs.

6. If there is a technique used on every page (machine sewing for example), complete this on each page at the same time."

DECEMBER
Designer: Alison Docherty

SUPPLIES
Patterned paper (Karen Foster Design); Cardstock (Prism); Ribbon (Making Memories); Die-cut letters; Thread

Templates **Here are some handy quick templates to add to your scrapbook pages**

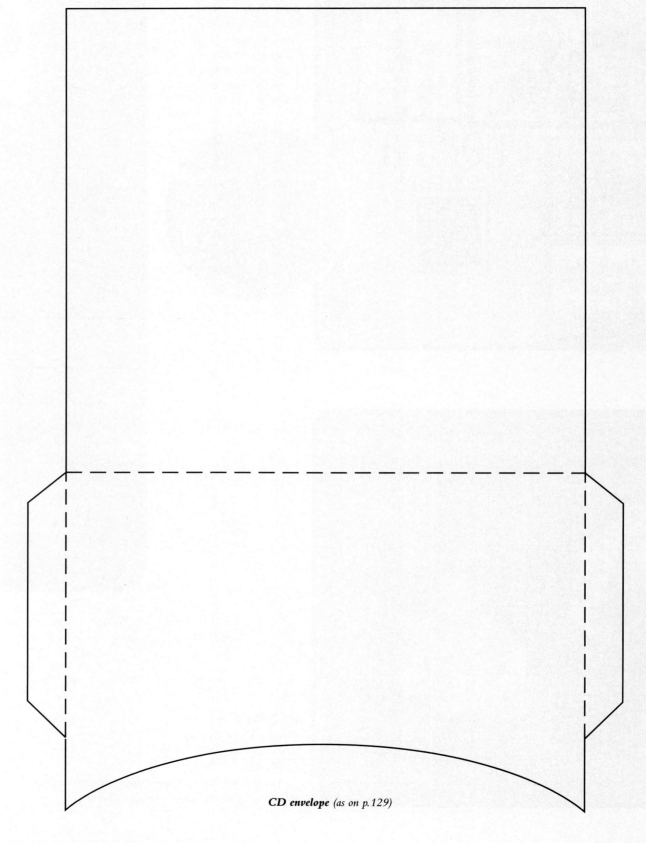

CD envelope *(as on p.129)*

Slide mount

Journaling tag

Pocket *(as on p. 49)*

Sketches

We can sometimes find ourselves with time on our hands but no inspiration! If this is the case, we recommend using sketches or plans to kick-start those creative processes

Much like an architect would draw out the idea and use it as a template for the finished building, many scrapbookers find it useful to sketch a visual placement of where photos, paper, journaling and embellishments will go. They can then file the sketch to use at a later date, or use it as a template to start their layout.

Quick tip

Once the sketch has been completed, a clever trick is to create three further layout ideas simply by rotating your sketch 90 degrees

You can use sketches time and time again, as they will look completely different with alternative colour schemes, paper, photos and embellishments. As they are square, sketches can easily be scaled up or down to suit the size of album you need – 12x12, 8x8 or 6x6.

If you are really stuck for inspiration, you could even lift the placement of elements from other people's work. There are also some great online sites that provide original sketches and layout ideas. Check out **www.scrap-maps.com** for a comprehensive range of templates to fit one or more photos.

But before you go anywhere else, see the template sketches on the following pages that we have put together for you to use. Why not try creating a complete album using a sketch per layout?

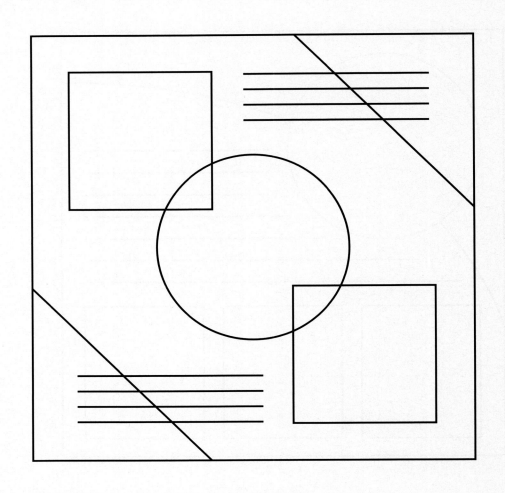

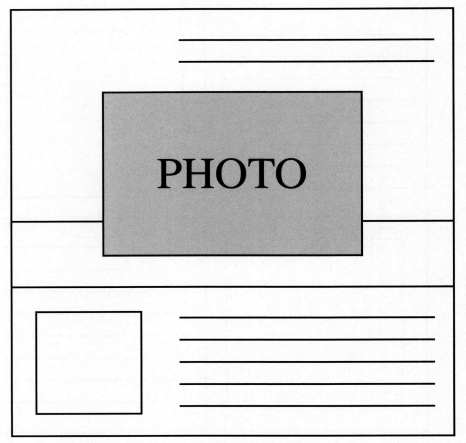

Scrapbooking A-Z

Layout A page design or the grouping of scrapbooking pages that go together. A layout can be one page, two pages or even a panoramic four-page spread.

Letter templates Plastic or metal templates in the shape of letters of the alphabet.

Lightbox A small light table used for embossing or viewing negatives.

Lightfast Coloured material that resists fading even when exposed to natural or artificial light.

Lignin A naturally occurring acid substance in wood that breaks down over time. Paper with lignin is not suitable for archival scrapbooking projects.

Magnetic album A photo album which uses a special adhesive to hold photographs in place and creates static for the plastic page cover to cling to. These are not suitable for scrapbooking.

Matt A surface that has no lustre or glossy finish.

Matting Matting is a technique that allows you to enhance your photos by adding a border around the outside edges. The border is, most often, made from an acid-free paper that looks almost like a frame. Matting is also a non-permanent way of cropping your pictures.

Memorabilia Certificates, documents and other items that tell a story. Memorabilia can include souvenirs from trips and mementoes from special occasions or historical events.

Memory or keepsake album Alternative terms for a scrapbook.

Monochromatic colour scheme Employing different values of the same colour.

Mount To adhere a photograph, embellishment or other item to another piece of paper.

Mounting squares A small square of double-sided tape-like adhesive dispensed from boxes.

Mulberry paper This paper is made from long fibres that create a feathered look when torn. It's available in various textures, weights, and colours.

Muted colours Subdued tints or shades of colours that tend to be more suitable for backgrounds.

Neutral A pH of 7.0. It is not acidic.

Oval cutters Paper trimmers that cut paper and photographs into ovals.

Page protectors Acid-free plastic sheets that display and protect pages.

Paper piecing Die-cuts or punches added together to create an image for your scrapbook page.

Paper tearing A technique in scrapbooking where you tear paper, rather than cutting it, to create a unique texture.

Paper trimmer Paper-cutting tool. Can be a rotary blade, or guillotine action.

Perforated punches Shapes that the scrapbooker can use as embellishments on a page by punching out along the perforations.

Permanent Stands the test of time and resists chemical breakdown. Also can mean unmovable.

pH level Measurement that tells a scrapbooker how acidic something is. For scrapbooking, you want to use products with a pH level of 7.0 or above.

Photo corners Paper with adhesive on the back used to stick photographs to a page by the corners, allowing you to attach them without applying adhesive directly to the photograph.

Photo safe Acid and lignin free.

Pigma pen A pen with special pigment that is acid free and permanent.

Polypropylene, polyethylene and polyester Stable plastics which are safe for photographs.

Post-bound albums Scrapbooking albums that are held together with metal posts that run through the pages.

Punch 1. A tool used to create small shapes. 2. The shapes created by the tool.

QuicKutz A brand of portable personal die-cutting systems. You buy die templates, and the tool will cut them out for you.

Repositionable A type of adhesive that can be stuck on paper, pulled back off and re-stuck as necessary.

Scrapbooking The creative art of displaying your photos and memorabilia. Can incorporate journaling and embellishments. The primary purpose of scrapbooking is to preserve memories for future generations, but a secondary purpose often is to exercise your creativity as you display your memories in a scrapbook.

Scrap lift To use an idea for part or whole of a page layout you've seen someone else use.

Self-healing mat A mat that can be repeatedly cut and still retains its form.

Serendipity squares Squares made by creating a torn collage of scraps on a background paper, then cutting it into squares and mounting onto complementary cardstock.

Setter A tool used to attach eyelets.

Shabby chic A style of scrapbooking that includes sanding, crumpling and distressing paper to give an old and worn look to your page.

Sizzix A brand of personal die-cutting systems.

Spiral-bound books Albums that are secured with a metal or plastic spiral binding running up the spine of the album.

Stencil A plastic pre-cut template used to trace and cut shapes. Usually used on paper or photos. They may also be used to apply paint or chalk to a surface in a contrasting colour.

Sticker A decorative adhesive-backed embellishment. Ranging in size from a few centimetres to a full page.

Tape roller A device that distributes tape on the back of photographs and scrapbooking pages. (Hermafix is a brand of tape roller.)

Template A stencil used to trace shapes onto scrapbook pages or photos.

Theme The overall idea or emphasis of a page/scrapbook.

Top loading An album or sheet protector in which your scrapbook page slides into your book from the top.

Tote A bag or hard case you carry or pull on wheels to transport your scrapbooking supplies.

Vellum A lightweight, translucent paper.

Walnut ink A photo-safe ink that gives an aged effect to your embellishments.

X-acto knife A super sharp hobby tool with a #11 blade used to cut intricate details.

Xyron machine A machine that creates stickers by applying an adhesive to cut-outs. Also makes magnets, or laminations.

Zig A brand of water-based marker.

Meet the design team

Without these designers, this book would not have been possible. We have great pleasure in introducing the creative team involved...

A TALENTED BUNCH... FROM THE UK

Mandy Anderson

Mandy has been scrapbooking for four years and is as passionate today about her hobby as she was when she first discovered it. She spends all her waking hours thinking and breathing scrapbooking. She scrapbooks from the heart and adores creating projects that highlight photographs and capture memories.

Paul Browning

Paul is self-employed and lives in Manchester with his partner. A member of both a local arts and scrapping group, Paul has scrapbooked for three years, producing albums ranging from pets to family history. "My current passion is altered art."

Nicola Clarke

Mother of two, Nicola has been scrapbooking for five years. With albums galore, she runs a local crop and works with scrapbooking part-time. "I can't think of any other way I would rather document our family moments and memories!"

Alison Docherty

Alison is a full-time occupational therapist, mother and wife. "My style is contemporary and I love to mix textures and patterns together." She is also a regular contributor to *Scrapbook Magazine*, *Papercraft Essentials* and *Simply Cards & Papercraft*.

Becks Fagg

"I love chic, simple and achievable scrapbooking. I *love* to write, which spills into my layouts. I'm a busy mum of four, and I like to keep my hands busy and the camera clicking!"

Michelle Grant

Managing Editor of Practical Publishing, Michelle loves a simple style, with photos and journaling the most important elements of her work. Mum to four children, Michelle enjoys cooking and eating!

Anne Hafermann

An avid cardmaker and stamper for many years, Anne shifted her focus to scrapbooking five years ago. "Since the birth of my son in 2004, scrapbooking has become a part of my daily life. My love of photography fuels my scrapping passion and my style is very eclectic."

Anita MacDonald

Married to Dale and mum to two wonderful girls, Anita has discovered the delights of many a patterned paper, metal embellishment and her biggest passion – blossoms! "I stand by my motto of 'anything goes'. I have started to teach scrapbooking locally and really enjoy introducing new crafters to this wonderful pastime. I love the outlet that scrapping gives me, allowing me to express myself – it's good therapy!"

Natalie O'Shea

Editor of *Scrapbook Magazine* and co-founder of the Scrappers Paradise retreat company, Natalie is married to Damon and has two boys, Ethan and Kian, who are the subject and inspiration for most of her work.

Debi Potter

Until recently, Debi made her living as an illustrator, producing designs for children's books, magazines and the greetings card industry. She now works for Ellison as one of their designers, where she has the luxury to be able to make cards all day long!

Sue Roberts

Sue lives on the south coast with her three cats. She was introduced to scrapbooking two years ago by another of our design team, Anita. "I am now hooked and love to scrap every spare minute of my time. My favourite subjects are animals, not only my cats but wild animals too. I am always visiting my local zoo."

Katie Shanahan-Jones

Katie lives in Oxfordshire with her husband and three children. "I've always crafted, starting with sewing and knitting. In 2002 I discovered scrapbooking and a passion began, and I have to say it has changed my life. I scrapbook most days and always have a project on the go!"

Kirsty Wiseman

Kirsty has been scrapping for just over 18 months. "I have a fascination with patterned papers and beautiful photographs, and I'm obsessed with colour, texture and design. Luckily I have a beautiful daughter who I can scrap, which makes my hobby that little bit more enjoyable."

A TALENTED BUNCH... FROM THE US

Michelle Baker

"Being so busy with product design for Li'l Davis, as well as teaching classes, travelling to trade shows and raising my three children, I'm always looking for shortcuts to make the precious little time I do spend on my personal projects as productive as possible."

Shauna Berglund-Immel

Shauna is a talented member of the Hot Off The Press design team. Her sophisticated scrapbooking style has been featured in idea books such as *Design Elements* and top magazines like *Creating Keepsakes*. Shauna lives in Oregon with her husband and two children.

Jenni Bowlin

Jenni resides in Nashville, Tennessee with her husband and two young sons. She is a published designer and a Creating Keepsakes 2003 Hall of Fame winner. On any given day you can find Jenni updating her blog, organising classes for her website, or designing for Li'l Davis.

Mandi Coombs

Mandi can't live without her digital camera, flip-flops, ice cream, and her wonderfully supportive husband. When not working on an assignment, you'll find her hanging out with her husband, taking pictures, playing video games and watching sports. She has loved to scrapbook since her mom dragged her to her first scrapbook class 10 years ago, and feels incredibly lucky to get to scrapbook for a job.

Brenda Cosgrove

"I have always enjoyed trying different crafts, but once I was introduced to scrapbooking it quickly took over other hobbies. I enjoy it because it is a creative way to record my family's history. I love seeing the faces of my husband and my four children light up as they look at scrapbooks that were created especially for them."

Nena Earl

"I am a young busy mom of three boys aged four, three and one, and one girl born on January 18th 2006. They are the reason I began scrapbooking – I love capturing and preserving precious, zany and precocious moments of mine and my boys' lives. I want these moments to be remembered and saved for all to experience. I love the 'chase', both with the camera and the page, and look forward to capturing and sharing those moments that everyone should experience and enjoy."

Becky Fleck

Becky lives in the Stillwater Valley of Columbus, Montana. "I am a graphic designer, avid fly fisherman, and hopelessly addicted scrapbooker. Whether you scrapbook a moment that was a significant event or an everyday happening, an account of your memories in a scrapbook will tell your story for generations to come."

Kelly Goree

"I am a 2006 Memory Makers Master and my work has been published in a variety of idea books and magazines, including *Memory Makers*, *Creating Keepsakes*, *Simple Scrapbooks* and *Scrapbooks Etc.* I live in Shelbyville, Kentucky with my husband Hoyte and my darling three boys Ethan, Turner and Carson."

Michelle Hill

Michelle lives in Carlsbad, California with her husband and four children, and joined the Li'l Davis design team in the summer of 2005, where her unique style led her straight into product design. Her work combines an ability to spot trends in popular culture with an eye for vintage design.

Kim Kesti

"I'm what most folks would call a scrapbook addict! It's part of my life and part of who I am. With seven kids to chase around, I'm never lacking photographs – I think it's so important to preserve those memories and special little moments. I live in Phoenix, Arizona and thrive in all the heat and commotion, but it's a dream of mine to visit the UK."

Marla Kress

Marla lives in Pittsburgh, Pennsylvania with her wonderful family. "In my free time you're likely to find me being creative in my studio. Combining photography with art is a creative outlet that I devour on a daily basis – it's great for my body, mind and soul."

Theresa Lundström

Theresa lives in Sweden with her family. "I discovered scrapbooking in March 2003 and have been hooked ever since. It's the best hobby I've ever had, because it combines all my other hobbies and allows me to capture my children's lives at different stages, all the while passing on our family history."

Faye Morrow Bell

Faye is a 2003 Creating Keepsakes Scrapbook Hall of Fame winner and the author of *At Home: Scrapbooking with Faye Morrow Bell*. Faye lives in Charlotte, North Carolina with her husband, George and their daughter, Tyler. Faye began scrapbooking when her daughter, Tyler, was about eight months old.

Missy Neal

By day, Missy is an engineering manager for a high tech company, but by night she's an avid Scrapbooker. "I have been a collector of memorabilia all my life, and got hooked on scrapbooking a little over five years ago. For me, scrapbooking is a great way to release the stress of my day job, while at the same time creating treasured memories that will be passed down to future generations."

Rozanne Paxman

Rozanne is the CEO of Scrap Girls, an online source of digital scrapbooking, printable scrapbooking, cardmaking and papercrafting supplies, whose goal is to make it simple and fast for anyone to become a great digital scrapbooker.

Natasha Roe

Natasha has discovered that scrapbooking is the perfect way to combine and express the things she is most passionate about – photography, keeping family records, self-expression, painting, sewing, journaling and so much more. "Scrapbooking has become so much more than a hobby – it's a way of life."

Shalae Tippetts

Shalae Tippetts lives in Provo, Utah with her husband and two beautiful little girls. To find an outlet for her creativity and love for art, she started designing for Scrapbook.com's line of E-cuts. She later found her real love for digital scrapbooking and enjoyed the opportunity to use her graphic design skills. She is currently designing for ScrapGirls.com, and it's here that she finds real fulfilment in being creative and combining all her favourite art media to create lasting memories for her family.

Kellene Truby

Kellene lives in Wichita, Kansas with husband, Doug and son Quade. She is the creative director of Pinecone Press, and has taught at CHA Winter, CHA Summer and CKUs across the US. "Scrapbooking is a creative release for me and one that I thoroughly enjoy. There is nothing more captivating than selecting papers that co-ordinate, stickers that help accentuate my photos and embellishments that pull the whole page together."

JUNKITZ DESIGN TEAM

Teresa Collins

Candice Cook

Debbie Hill

Tim Holtz

Annette Lauts

Stacey Panassidi

Janna Wilson

Resources Guide

MAIN SPONSORS

All My Memories
www.allmymemories.com
Available in the UK through
ScrapGenie Ltd
www.scrapgenie.co.uk
Tel: 01440 704400

All My Memories started in 1996 as a retailer in Colorado and grew until the owner, Jorjana Brown, launched its own line of products in 2000 and the wholesale division of AMM was born. The company hasn't looked back since, winning industry awards and consistently creating refreshingly original and classically styled lines. Numbered amongst its innovations are Time Savers embossed cardstock sets, Mini Mementos and the Tote-ally Cool storage totes.

BasicGrey
www.basicgrey.com
Available in the UK through
ScrapGenie Ltd
www.scrapgenie.co.uk
Tel: 01440 704400

BasicGrey specialise in creating cutting-edge paper designs. The products reflect a raw and progressive design style built to stimulate and inspire. Inspiration and craftsmanship are combined to produce a portfolio of high quality, unique paper lines.

Daisy D's
www.daisydspaper.com
Available in the UK through
ScrapGenie Ltd
www.scrapgenie.co.uk
Tel: 01440 704400

Daisy D's has long been associated with artistic, approachable and fun designs. The latest ranges are perfect for altered art projects and have particular appeal to scrapbookers who love all things heritage or shabby chic. Beautiful rustic embellishments have recently been added to its ranges, as well as the super cool file folders, rub-ons and bare chipboard pieces.

Ellison Design
www.ellisondesign.com
Tel: 08706 000625

As the innovators behind the Sizzix brand, Ellison captured the hearts and minds of crafters everywhere. With the release of its newest

brand, Ellison leverages nearly three decades of tradition empowering creativity to offer a total crafting solution for today's crafter.

Hot Off The Press
www.craftpizazz.com
Available in the UK through
Craftime
www.craftime.co.uk
Tel: 01623 722828

Hot Off The Press is a leading manufacturer of scrapbooking and papercrafting in the US. Ever since the company began in 1980 with one self-published craft instruction book, HOTP has emphasised creativity, personal expression and the joy of crafting something handmade. Today it offers over 900 products that provide customers with innovative ideas and the tools to create them

with. In 25 years, HOTP has been honored with 26 craft industry Awards of Excellence!

Junkitz
www.junkitz.com
Available in the UK through
Scrapbook Trade
www.scrapbooktrade.co.uk
Tel: 01505 871332

The world of scrapbooking is constantly evolving and the creative team at Junkitz is dedicated to developing products that will help our customers unzip their imaginations. Its innovative line of products, including Paperz, Washerz, Gum Dropz, and Clipz, were designed with beginner, intermediate and advanced scrapbookers in mind.

Karen Foster Design
www.karenfosterdesign.com
Available in the UK through
ScrapGenie Ltd
www.scrapgenie.co.uk
Tel: 01440 704400

Karen Foster Design is one of the craft industry's most innovative

scrapbooking manufacturers. It has won several industry awards including: Creating Keepsakes Reader's Choice Award Best Themed Paper; Reader's Choice Award Finalist for both Patterned Paper and Stickers; and Craftrends Finalist for the Back to School Line, Clikit, Gels, and the Pet Line.

Li'l Davis Designs

Li'l Davis Designs
www.lildavisdesigns.com
Available in the UK through
ScrapGenie Ltd
www.scrapgenie.co.uk
Tel: 01440 704400

Tricia Barrett's love of scrapbooking led her to open Li'l Davis Designs in January, 2002. The company, a true family affair, is named after her five-year-old daughter, Davis, while her husband, Brian, serves as Senior Art Director. Since the introduction of its first product line of laser-cut shapes, the company has significantly expanded to include a complete line of embellishments, paper, templates, idea books and tools. A full service scrapbook company, Li'l Davis Designs has emerged as an industry leader, bringing high-quality, innovative products to the scrapbook market.

Pebbles Inc
www.pebblesinc.com
Available in the UK through

ScrapGenie Ltd
www.scrapgenie.co.uk
Tel: 01440 704400

Pebbles Inc is the manufacturing side of Pebbles in my Pocket, a chain of stores in Utah. It all began in 1992, when owner Brenda Birrell began organising her memories in scrapbooks. She quickly realised there was not one place to purchase supplies. She decided to create her own scrapbook business to fuel her creativity. A few years ago, the creative spirit took over as the company began manufacturing its own line of scrapbooking items. Pebbles Inc best-sellers include the market-leading chalk sets.

Sizzix
www.sizzix.com
Distributed in the UK by Ellison
www.ellison.com
Tel: 08706 000625

Once Ellison developed the technology for its die-cutting system, the Sizzix brand was launched in 2001. The Sizzix machine continues to be the tool of choice for a wide range of consumers – from aspiring creatives to professional artists – for its versatility and affordability.

OTHER MANUFACTURERS

7gypsies
www.7gypsies.com

American Crafts
www.americancrafts.com

Bazzill Basics
www.bazzillbasics.com

Chatterbox
www.chatterboxinc.com

ColorBox
www.clearsnap.com

Craft Robo
www.graphtecgb.com
Tel: 01978 666700

Doodlebug Design
www.doodlebug.ws

EK Success
www.eksuccess.com

K&Co
www.kandcompany.com

Magic Mesh
www.magicmesh.com

Magic Scraps
www.magicscraps.com

Making Memories
www.makingmemories.com

PaperArtsy
www.paperartsy.co.uk
Tel: 01277 212911

Pioneer Albums
www.pioneerphotoalbums.com

Prima
www.primamarketinginc.com

Prism Paper
www.prismpaper.com

Provo Craft
www.provocraft.com

QuicKutz
www.quickutz.com

Ranger Industries
www.rangerink.com

Rusty Pickle
www.rustypickle.com

Scrapbook Sally
www.scrapbooksally.com

Scrapworks
www.scrapworks.com

sei
www.shopsei.com

Tsukineko
www.tsukineko.com

Woodware Craft Collection Ltd
Tel: 01756 700024

Xyron
www.xyron.com

ZipeMate
www.zipemate.com

Final word

How do you cram a completed scrapbook album into a weekend? Well, the same way I managed to cram in this book while having baby number four, organising a trade show and a few other major family events – you prioritise!

I am all about putting first things first, and making a point of using my time to reflect what is most important to me. When I want to finish a task I put it to the top of the list (and the list is long), and I make the time and make it a priority. I juggle my tasks every day and occasionally a weekend is exactly what I need to refocus, regroup and refresh.

If you want to give yourself a break, and also give yourself some time, give yourself a weekend to scrapbook your memories. Whether on your own or with friends (I would highly recommend the latter) – make a date! Plan to achieve something that no amount of messy kids or dishes in the sink will take away. Plan on creating something that lasts!

Use some of the ideas our talented team have shared – there is a common thread in their own design secrets, so take advantage of their experience and prove them right!

So find the time, make the time and scrapbook – this weekend (or next)!

Becs!